Singularity

Dialogues on artificial intelligenc

MIEKE MOSMULLER

SINGULARITY

Dialogues on artificial intelligence and spirituality

OCCIDENT • PUBLISHERS

Translated from Dutch by
Ruth Franssen
and
Sebastian Tombs

Band MM 54

Occident Publishers
Post box 306
5110 AH Baarle Nassau
The Netherlands
Phone: 0031 - 13 - 5079948 E-mail: info@occidentpublishers.com
Website: www.occidentpublishers.com

Cover image: Carina van den Bergh
Graphic design: Carina van den Bergh

ISBN/EAN: 978-90752-4060-3

Sometimes it feels as though nature brings together the full range of human potentialities, into a single hereditary disposition. Usually each human child receives a small portion of this greater whole, and we all complement one another. But, occasionally, the whole universe seems to be poured into one child. The wonderful thing is that when you look at the parents of such a child, most often you wouldn't say that they were particularly talented people and yet, together, they have conceived a child that will present extraordinary intelligence on the one hand, or have an artistic aptitude that could open the way to the concert stage - or even both.

Thus, in an ordinary city in 'middle of the road' Netherlands in temperate Europe, a little boy was born. During the first few months there seemed to be nothing special about the baby. It slept and drank and cried - like all babies do and, later on, smiled kindly upon the world. It was the parents' first child, so they had no comparison. They did not find it strange that, after a year this little boy started to speak words and make sentences, even before he was able to walk properly. They didn't pay much attention, either, to the fact that the boy was singing songs that he heard on television, while other children didn't have any words at all. He was a late walker, but that also wasn't very remarkable. His father taught at a primary school and his mother was a secretary in a large company, so the little boy was taken to a nursery early on. There, it was striking how quickly the child could talk and how awake he was, how much joy he had in doing small jobs. He wanted to get on! As small as he was. Learning seemed to be the greatest joy in his young life …

It only really became clear how gifted he was in observing, paying attention, learning, when he went to pre-school at the age of four. It didn't take long before the parents were invited to come to the school for a talk. In the meantime, two more sisters had been born who did not show such noteworthy development at all. Of course, the parents

7

did see the difference and they were happy about it. Apparently, their child was highly gifted …

At the school the boy went to, people had an eye for this phenomenon of exceptional giftedness. That is why it was immediately noticed. Thus, the question was discussed with the parents: 'How will we deal with this in the future? Should we slow down his eagerness to learn and ensure that he can stay at the same level as his peers? Or is it better for him that we stimulate his keenness to learn and offer him a whole range of development opportunities?'

In consultation, parents and teachers came to the conclusion that this gifted child should be stimulated as much as possible. For example, he was given piano lessons at the age of four. The teacher who taught him was amazed at the child's ability to imitate simple melodies immediately, to make the notation his own and to practise one piece to the next perfectly.

At school he learned to read and write at the age of four, and at the age of five he was already reading simple books. He would sit at home in the room on the couch reading the umpteenth book from the library. And he read, and he read, and he read …

At five he started at primary school and it was soon agreed that he should skip a year. When he was in the third grade it was decided that he could again skip a year. So the little boy flew through the school years on the wings of his potential. His parents didn't realize that they might have to try to prevent him from setting himself above his peers because of his abilities. They were proud of him - they showed that, and they didn't notice that their pride became his own, too.

When he was given a book to read, he tended to go straight to the last page. When he got a new piano book, he tried to play the last piece in the book right away. If he got new textbooks at school then he did the same thing: he tried to skip everything and see if he could solve the problems at the end of the book. As long as it was about arithmetic, he succeeded. With languages he also succeeded. But the more substantive subjects, needless to say, require you to get involved. He didn't like to read a history book … So then his parents would seek out a video or some kind of program so he could record the content he had to learn, quickly and pleasantly. Patience wasn't exactly taught on these intellectual journeys … He was a real child of the bird's-eye view. If he had to think about something for any length of time in order to grasp it, he soon lost interest.

He didn't really have much patience with his playmates. As a matter of course, he took the lead in their games and didn't take kindly to opposition. He had to be the boss, be in charge of setting the rules, and had little sense for what other children in the game actually wanted. Yet he had many friends, all boys but for a single girl. The children admired his inventiveness, they enjoyed his humour, his jokes, his attention and his ideas. They gladly surrendered to all that and gave him the leadership he so desperately craved.

Of course, it is clear that if you are such a boy in whom nature apparently desires to enable great achievements later in life, then you are mainly concerned with your own development. The parents didn't perceive that they, too, were full of admiration for their gifted child and were unaware that they should restrain him or teach him a certain moral depth. They were convinced that in this miracle child everything was well – yes, the best; and that, as parents, they merely had to watch in amazement as to how all this would unfold.

With a loud bang he closed his laptop.
"What's wrong with you?!" snapped his girlfriend, irritated.
"This isn't going to work at all! I want to write about how I grew up, and it's going to be a completely lifeless, meaningless story."
"How far have you got?"
"I've written about my very first years, about kindergarten, primary school - but it's nothing, it's not about anything. It's got nothing to do with me at all!"
"But didn't you write from your own experience?"
"Experience? What experience! I just want to write down the facts… What it's like when you are born a child prodigy and then you go to

school, what you go through there, how people treat you, what you learn, what you don't learn, your irritations, your impatience, the lack of people who understand what you are talking about … "

"But why would you want to write all that down? Who would benefit from that?"

"Why? Because I think it's interesting for a lot of people to see how a child prodigy like that doesn't end up being something very special … "

"Well," Els said, "you are earning tons every year … "

"But that's not what I'm talking about, that's not what I mean. If I really were a prodigy that had blossomed, I'd have two billion a year. But I don't care about the money, I'm talking about the fact that what was apparently to have been great riches turns out to be pretty modest, after all."

"You really are crazy! How so 'modest'!? You've got a fantastic job, you've done three university courses at the same time, you've graduated with distinction in all three, you've got a PhD, you've got this great job, you can play the piano like a concert pianist - and it's still not good enough?"

"There are so many people who graduate with great grades and get a great job and play a musical instrument. That's not special."

"Yeah, but you are really special: you know that."

He sighed.

"I don't know. I want to write down what it's been like to have always had the feeling that you can do things in the best possible way - that there's an expectation that you're going to do great things - and that by the time you're 34, you find out that life is all very normal, in fact. Not special at all, no celebrity! Besides, I have the feeling that my capacities are becoming less rather than more, I don't feel like I'm still develop-ing. That was how I felt when I was at school and university, but after that … I've got a job, a steady girlfriend, maybe we'll have some kids. What's so special about that?"

Els put her phone down and gave him all her attention. Initially, her emotions had been partly engaged with her Facebook messages. Now she began to take notice that this was really serious.

"Well, what did you expect?"

He looked thoughtfully in front of him.

"They always gave me the impression that I would reach the top."

"But you have reached it, haven't you?"

"No, I haven't. What I really want is for those predictions of where I would get to by age 34, to come true. Not that I'd just have to be satisfied with some expensive flat, with a girlfriend and a good income!"

"So - now you were going to write. Then why don't you get on with it? Maybe that'll help, and while you're writing you'll come to an understanding of what you want to do in life."

"That's not why I started writing. I started writing because I thought: a life story like this is interesting for other people."

"So at least you could become famous that way?"

"Maybe that's it … it's just hard to accept that you've not achieved more with all those great talents they've always said you had."

"Why don't you tell me what you actually want to write? Maybe it'll get livelier because you'll be telling someone who really cares about you, is interested in you. Someone who wants you to be okay."

"I'll give it a try … " he said hesitantly.

"I think it's important that you describe what you've been through, how you've actually felt things."

"That's the feminine aspect; I'm more focused on the facts."

"You've got a feminine aspect yourself, you know! Otherwise you wouldn't be so dissatisfied right now. Dissatisfaction is also perception. Tell me what you were going to entrust to paper … "

He sorted out his laptop, sat down on a chair, took a deep breath and got ready to start.

Els sat down on the couch and remembered just in time to turn on her iPhone to record the conversation. Maybe, in the end, this could one day serve as the basis for a biographical novel?

"Tell all!" she said invitingly, and so he began.

"You know, when you're a child, you obviously don't realize there's something special about you. You really wouldn't have that inner realisation yourself, you know, because the adults around you keep emphasising the fact that you can do everything better than the other children. Whether that is so good for a child is questionable – because, while it may not make you conceited, at the minimum it can make you more proud of yourself. There was no hiding the fact that I could learn so quickly, was so eager to learn, so musical, so technical, so handy, so artistic, gifted, interested in everything and yet cheerful and, in some ways, also quite social. In short, a child who seemed to be a gifted all-rounder …

"Again, I wouldn't have realised that, if it hadn't been constantly repeated, and that flattery - or praise - did, naturally, stimulate me to continue to be ambitious and to try to do everything I came across along my way as well and as quickly as possible. I took every available book I could from the library and I don't think I'm exaggerating when I say I was fed up with the world by the time I was nine….. I had explored the plant kingdom, I got to know the whole animal world, I knew the minerals, the gems, the metals; I learned about the periodic table of the elements, I found out about the various geological strata of the earth in connection with the development periods in history. I read about meteorology, about the formation of clouds, of rain, wind, storm, ebb, flow, atmospheric changes, causes of earthquakes and of volcanic eruptions. I read books about history, first about the Netherlands, later of Europe, of Greece, of Rome, but also of Asia, of Mexico, America. Everything I could find to read, I absorbed. I tried to find out about the peoples of the earth and, you have to appreciate, everything I discovered was on paper and on television. I also learned a lot by watching documentary films. Imagine, a boy of 7 or 8 years old who is studying science at university student level …

"My parents just let me have my way. I don't remember them ever trying to hold me back, or saying: 'Now, you shouldn't watch movies for a month', or 'You should stop taking books out of the library for a while', or 'You shouldn't study piano for two hours every day!' I had an indescribable drive to learn and develop, and I wouldn't want to say that it wasn't something special or that it wasn't good, because I was very happy with it. I've always had the feeling, that the whole future is open, because you can go on learning, all through your life.

"But, as I said, at nine years old, I was tired of the earth and I wanted to move on. So I took on the universe! First, I was exploring the constellations in space. Later I also tried to grasp the movement of the planets and the position of the stars in the night sky. My father and mother knew nothing about these things, had no knowledge of them at all. This knowledge also had to be obtained entirely from books and from scientific programmes and films. I saved up for a star calendar, and for a telescope to be able to view the stars better. And then there came a moment when the question for me was: What is the history of the Universe? I had studied the history of the earth as it is known in science, now I wanted to get to know the scientific history of the universe as it could be found in books. I familiarised myself with the usual ideas about the origin of the Universe. I didn't have any critical questions. I don't think that's appropriate for that primary school age, in any case. You record what's on offer and save it, as it were, on your internal hard wiring … "

"Oh-oh!" exclaimed Els.

"Well, you try to remember," he smiled, "but you don't have the inclination to ask questions in the sense of: Is this actually true? As you know, my parents have no religious feeling or thoughts at all. They consider themselves liberal materialists, and I was brought up with the motto: 'Try to get the best and the most out of this life, because it's the only one you've got'. I wouldn't say that they said that all the time, but they lived like that - and for me it was an unspoken permission to gather as much knowledge as possible.

"Now, of course, as a primary school child, even if you are highly gifted, you don't have all the knowledge capacity that an adult has. A university degree in astronomy would perhaps have been too much to ask for of, let's say, a 12-year-old child. But in a popular scientific way I did approach that knowledge, and so then it does make it difficult to endure the laborious everyday progress of acquiring knowledge in high school.

"I was already in grammar school by the age of 11, and it brought me new and intriguing subjects. For example, I found the study of Latin extremely interesting. Not so much because of the meaning of the words or the content of the texts we learned to read. Much more because of the remarkable grammatical constructions Latin has and which are so different from our modern languages. The teacher of classical languages noticed that I had a feeling for this and started to express his amazement loud and clear: 'This boy has an innate talent for detecting the logic of language in grammatical forms!!!' he told my parents. My father wrote it down, and told me later. I didn't really understand what he meant, but I did feel it vaguely, because that's exactly why that old classical language of Latin interested me so much. Because the coherence of the concepts lay much more in the construction of the language than is the case with our later, modern languages, in which everything is rolled out word for word.

"I found Greek to be an even more mysterious language….Well, this is also due to the different alphabet, the different characters, whose sounds you hear as though through a veil. I found the grammar in Greek much more artistic than in Latin, but therefore also less interesting. Maybe it is true that in Latin, when we get to know that language these days, everything that people have thought with that language is somehow locked up in it? When you think that the all-encompassing wisdom of the Catholic Church has been thought of in Latin, it gives you goose bumps….."

Els interrupted his flow of words and said:

"Yes, but that's almost a spiritual insight, isn't it? It's not normal for you to say something like that! How can you imagine that something that is not recorded - yes, in writing and in words, but not in the language itself - because people have thought Catholic wisdom in that language, that that sticks to it? How am I to imagine, as a modern human being, that when you learn Latin, you can experience that Catholic wisdom in it? In the language itself?"

He gazed thoughtfully ahead, and said:

"Yes, of course, I've argued with myself on this several times, and yet… I wasn't raised Catholic, I've never been to a Catholic Mass or anything like that, I hardly know any Catholic priests - and that's precisely why it's so surprising that I've felt something in the Latin language from the very beginning which - I later learned - is Catholic wisdom! For me, that's a fact. How that is to be explained is something else, I don't comprehend that either; but for me, it is a fact."

"Interesting … " Els said and she meant it. "But I do wonder: where was all this happening? It sounds like the development of an indoor world that has no context. Of course, you talk about your parents and about your teachers, but where did this happen? Did you play outside - and where was that? Did you learn to ice skate, did you go walking in the rain, did you fall down and scrape your knees, did you get your head handed to you by the teacher because you were chatting during class, what did the playground look like, what did you do there, did you go to school all day, did you stay over or did you go home at lunchtime? How was your life beyond just the content of books and watching movies?"

He looked at her in surprise, and said:

"But you know that part of my life, don't you? We've talked about it so many times! Surely you know that I don't just live indoors!"

"Yes, I know, but I thought we were having this conversation - an autobiographical conversation - that could be engaging for other people. So far, I'm seeing an extremely smart and perhaps also very sweet little boy….. but it has no environment."

"Good, good … " he said, and it flashed through his mind that, of course, as always, she was right again. Because the emphasis in his childhood was on life in the content of books and films and the joy and development based on learning, and being aware that you're good at it. When he looked back at his childhood, all this was indeed very much in the foreground. What Els was asking about now, about the environment, he had to pull it in, as it were, by force! To be sure, he had his memories of those surroundings, but in essence they played a much less prominent role …

"Good, good … " he repeated, and began to elaborate.

"Well, the environment in which all this took place is the big city of Amsterdam. That's where I was born, that's where I grew up, that's where I partly studied -"

"Partly?" she asked. "I thought you did all your studying in Amsterdam?"

"By 'partly' I mean - you know, I did three courses at the same time - two of them here in Amsterdam and the third in Delft. I've lived in Amsterdam my whole life and, as you know, I am still living here. I know the city well."

"But where were you born? In what part of the city?"

"I was born in one of the streets around Churchill Avenue; in a house which is typical in Amsterdam, a 'double upper' house. It's not an ordinary apartment, but it's not an ordinary house either, it's half a house plus an upstairs; with its own stairs, its own front door. Nobody comes in through that front door except the person who lives in that house. That's where I was born and that's where I grew up and that's where I lived until I met you and moved in with you.

"The days when you could just play outside had passed. It was far too crowded, there were far too many cars - and far too many weird characters on the street. My mother thought they might hurt me. Although there were still children playing in the street, I certainly didn't participate. I went to a community school, there was a large fenced playground and I always enjoyed playing there with my classmates. Sometimes I got into fights, but most of all I romped, played games, teased the teachers and did all those things that kids do in their free time. But I was always very happy when the bell rang and I could go home and get on with my projects … "

"Did you have any friends with whom you did that?" Els asked.

"Okay, I understand that you want to portray me as 'the gifted child with no social environment', but it really wasn't like that! I've always managed to interest my peers or my classmates in my projects, and although they were more of suppliers of information - I mean, they went to the library for me, or they looked for certain films for me, and we watched them together, and we shared that experience together. It was only the interest of my friends that ended when they left my house, and that's when a project really came into its own! In that sense you could say that I was a lonely child … And yet I never felt it like that. When I recall my childhood experiences, I feel a huge gratitude for the happiness I enjoyed in my youth. Parents who set me free… teachers who admired me… friends who looked up to me … "

"They must have been jealous of you too, right?"

"That might have been so … ", he replied. "I didn't really notice that, perhaps because of my strong inner world, so I didn't perceive exactly what was going on out there. But if they had really been jealous, they would have reacted differently to me - and I never noticed that!

"But I did have to leave my friends behind. Skipping a year twice means having to get used to a whole new class environment. I do recall having to live up to the fact that the children viewed me with some

16

distrust. 'What kind of braggart or trickster or show-off?', or something like that. It took a couple of months before I had gained their confidence. But I did get that trust."

"All right," Els said. "Now I know a little more about your outside world. But I'm still wondering: did you have any experiences of nature, too - or have you only seen houses and paving stones?"

"My experience of nature was, indeed, mainly from books on nature. My parents did go camping every summer and then, of course, I had to go with them. We'd set up camp in the midst of nature with a tent for three, four, sometimes even five weeks, and then I'd have plenty of opportunity to see what I'd learned about in the books, in the open air."

"So, you actually had some knowledge first, and only later the experience of observing it?"

"In the big picture, yes. But in everyday life, of course, you see everything first and then you think: what is this? You hear what it is, you are taught that and then you recognize it from that moment on. But I had read a lot about classifying plants and animals, so when I was standing next to the tent on the grass and watching everything grow and blossom – yes, then my knowledge added to what I saw. And I can tell you that this is a great happiness in my life: that I know so much, that I recognize so much. Actually, of course, my desire is to know absolutely everything, and then recognise everything … '

"That's impossible - what you're saying!"

"Needless to say, at this moment, it is still impossible. But - if you live by the principle that you are only on this earth once, why shouldn't you strive to get to know as much of this earth as possible?"

Els said, bemused:

"That's weird, what you're saying now! If you only live once on this earth, why would that make you want to get to know everything? Who else would benefit? Why would that be? You'll be gone at some point! You were born with a wonderful giftedness…. you spend your whole life gathering knowledge - for what? You die, and all is gone."

Els understood the art of silencing him, over and over again. Sometimes he thought: 'She's actually the gifted one. Her knowledge goes far beyond mine. She doesn't know that much - although she knows a lot of things that I don't know - but with that lesser knowledge it seems as if she sees further, while I am near-sighted. I can see all the details, but I can't see into the distance. She looks with the greatest ease past all the close-up details and sees the bigger perspectives in the distance!'

He didn't say that to her, as he didn't want to disrupt the balance in which they lived. Although he sometimes felt that he was not being honest about it.

They took a break. He made an espresso for them both. They walked around a bit, took a look at the messages on their phones, and a bit at the news, and then decided to carry on with the conversation.

"Feel free to ask critical questions," he said. "It helps me to formulate better what a life like mine actually looks like now."

"Okay ... " and she started right away. "You told me how, when you were camping, you could enjoy everything that grows and blossoms and that you could identify them from your extensive study of the different species of plants. But I'm still not sensing the feeling of the sun on your bare back, the grass tickling your feet, the smell of the grass after the rain, the effect of the starry sky when it's pitch black, that creepy feeling when you have to walk a little way across the campsite in that pitch dark to go to the toilet. I'm also missing those sort of things when you've been describing your life at home and at school. These everyday things that make life worth living!"

He smiled at her and said:

"It's just a question of what you choose to describe. It's precisely what you've described - of course I've had these sensations and I still have them! When we're walking to the cinema together in the evening bustle of Amsterdam, I really am not thinking about the number of frames per second that make a film; as I sense you beside me in that cosy hustle and bustle of the city, I'm looking forward to sitting next to you in the cinema - whatever film is showing!"

She smiled too, and said:

"Yes, you're sweet, I know that! But I'm trying to get an impression of the values that are at work in your life. What was really important?"

"Yes ... then to be honest, I have to admit that those feelings of the wet grass on my feet were drowned out by that compendium of human knowledge. But that's wonderful, isn't it? Once you've felt wet grass on your feet, you know what it feels like! I don't need that repetition, I can recall it from memory … "

Els interrupted him:

"That sounds slightly arrogant, or maybe more than slightly arrogant!"

"Why?" he asked in amazement. "I'm not bigging myself up, I'm just describing what you're asking me to. Namely: what are my core life values? Yes, they really do lie in the accumulation of knowledge and in the ever-increasing overview of what a human being in the world, and the world around him, actually is."

"Do you really have the idea, then," she asked, "that the more extensive your knowledge becomes, the better you can encompass that?"

"Certainly," he answered without hesitation. "When I consider what I now know of the universe, and of the tiniest particles - that are also the smallest particles in a human body - and if I compare that to what I knew about it at grammar school, it's obvious that I know a lot more about it now."

"And the 'Riddle of Man', for example - that the more science knows, the more it appreciates the vastness of what it doesn't know…?" she asked, "Hasn't that area of the 'not known' grown any bigger?"

"No, not at all!" he said definitively.

She took a deep breath and said:

"Well, I don't understand any of that. As you know, I'm currently learning Italian on one of those apps on my phone and I've noticed that learning actually consists of gathering as much vocabulary as possible. The more words you know, the more you are at home in the area of the language you're wanting to learn."

"But that's nonsense, really. If you don't also learn verbs and conjugations and the coherence of grammar, then you are still dealing with a completely dead part of such a foreign language."

"You see," she said, "here you see it! Here you see that you can increase your knowledge endlessly and yet you do not empathize with the living essence of the language!"

"And what corresponds in that example to the 'Riddle of Man and the Universe'?"

"The analogy is that with your gigantic memory you have accumulated an enormous amount of knowledge, which is comparable to learning words. How all these different facts that you know are connected as a living whole – well, I believe the one can improve the other!"

He felt some indignation rising, and said:

"Of course, it really isn't like that. That so-called 'knowing' that you're talking about, of all those facts, that's a kind of knowing in which those facts are truly interconnected, they're not all distinct and separate from each other! The relationships between these facts, then, lies in an area comparable with the grammatical connections in a language. I would really dispute that all I know is facts. I have carried out in-depth studies that actually consist, in their entirety, of obtaining coherence between facts."

"Okay … " she said. "That's clearly your point of view, then. I see it differently, but we'll come to that in the course of our further conversation."

He laughed and said:

"As if it's something new between us, what's coming up here! We've talked about it so many times…. and I expect we'll talk about it many more times yet."

"Let's move on. You went to a school with an academic focus. Which one in Amsterdam?"

"Yes, it was obvious that I was going to go to a grammar school in our neighbourhood. It was and still is close by. It was within easy walking distance, so to speak. But I always cycled. That's the Vossius Gymnasium. I had a strange time there. Because I was two years younger than my classmates they treated me like a younger brother. Very affectionately, respectful of my achievements, too, but not as someone who could really fit in with the social life of the class. They took me with them as a younger brother, but then I wasn't taken seriously. The girls thought I was a child and I have to say that I myself was not very interested in the phenomenon 'girl'. Of course, I did go to the class parties but I didn't feel like I really wanted to take part in what was customary at those parties. So, I was mainly an observer. I considered everything with great interest, but I didn't feel like a participant."

"That sounds painful!" Els said.

"Yes, when I look back at it from an adult point of view, I find it painful, too. But it didn't feel painful at all at the time. I felt at home in that class, they were nice to me, I could tag along. I was interested in everything. I was never the kind of gifted child who gets bored doing other things in class. I have always been very interested in people, for example: the types of teachers. I wrote down in a book certain character-traits of the different teachers in the different classes; I also made notes of which kind of pupils hated which kind of teachers, and which kind of pupils hated which kind of classes … "

"But what was the point!?" she exclaimed.

"I never wondered if it made any sense - but I did it because I was interested in discovering certain structures, maybe recognizing certain patterns in one case or the other - and then seeing whether they harmonized or not."

"And because you also know that such information makes a difference … ?"

"Oh certainly, even if it's not knowledge that can be represented exactly in a graph. I would have liked to have done that, but I didn't succeed. But I did get to know what makes a 'typical' maths teacher, a typical physics teacher, a typical teacher of classical languages and so on. Of course, it's in your genome what subject you choose, and that genome determines not only what subjects you choose, but also determines your whole being. So it seemed logical to me that there would be a connection."

"Oh help!" said Els, "The Genome!"

"We'll come back to that," said Els. "First, I have a number of other questions. Did you ever do anything with your hands, or did you just study up there in that upstairs room?"

"Yes, you know," he said, "I've done a lot with my hands. I mean, playing the piano for hours every day, that's activity with your hands, isn't it? A lot happened in the mind, yes. But I've also done other things, I may never have told you that? Ever since I was about 10, I had an irrepressible need to take apart devices and put them back together again."

"What?!?!"

"Yeah, that wasn't so much fun for my Mum and sometimes my Dad, because I took the coffee machine apart, I took the radio apart, I took the vacuum cleaner apart; and then I tried to find out how it all worked. Then I put it back together again. Most of the time it went well, but inevitably I also had my failures, in the sense that I had dismantled a device into all its myriad components, but then didn't really know how to put it back together anymore! Then there's only one thing you can do with it, and that's throw it away…. But mostly I had a fair idea about what I could or couldn't attempt. For example, I've never tried to take the phone apart even though it probably wouldn't have been that hard, but I didn't dare. Later, I did demolish the computer … I generally tried to get to know equipment by taking it apart and putting it back together again. In that way I got to know a great deal about technical matters … ”

"Yet again: 'got to know it'," she said.

"Yes, but what's your point? Why would I do crafts, just to do crafts… surely there's always some point in doing something?"

"Well, I'll have to think about that!" Els said. "I don't think it's true… … but maybe it's true for you. On the contrary, I love wasting my time on useless activities - such as painting my nails…"

"But that does have a purpose, too, which is to make your hands look nice and tidy and interesting afterwards."

"Well, it doesn't really make any sense to me, anyway. Or, for example, sitting in the sauna for an hour - why would I do that? Why would you do that? Just to investigate certain processes?!"

"I do it because I like it - and because I think it's also good for my body to stimulate the whole machinery from time to time; and yes, I do wonder what exactly happens in that 'machinery'. I'm going to look that up, too … ”

"Come to that, why didn't you go to medical school? You could have done that at the same time!"

"You're mocking me!" he said. "No, I understand that medical school takes up all of your time, so I did it differently. But - you had more questions?"

"Yes, especially about your piano playing. What else did you do with that? How did it develop?"

"It went very well. But it was a disappointment to find out that with my advanced piano playing I couldn't play in the student orchestra. A piano is out of place there. What I did then was ask some of my musically talented classmates or fellow students to form a quartet, a quintet. I succeeded in doing so, and I've really enjoyed playing together with them over the years and, as you know, we still do."

"It seems as though there's more than sixteen hours in each day of yours!"

"Well, I use my time very efficiently; I don't spend it on such useless things as painting my nails!"

"Then it came to your choice of subjects for your final school exams; you chose the beta set, I suppose?"

"Yes, of course, but the Classics teacher was so disappointed that he asked me if I didn't want to join his course at the same time -"

"And you did … "

"Indeed I did, and with great pleasure! While I had settled on my double final exams and it was an absolute certainty for me that I wanted to study science, I was still under the impression that it was necessary to get an idea of how, as a human being, you can look at your own ability to know - and that's why I thought it would be important to study philosophy also."

"So, what did you – really - want to become?"

" Yes … I wanted to be an inventor most of all, but it was not clearly defined what I would want to invent and in what field. But I was hoping that I could join the great inventors in the field of technology. When I went to university, the development of computer science was already in full swing, so it was obvious that I would choose that subject in any case. I was most interested in artificial intelligence, but I also wanted to study the biological sciences, in particular the exact biological, biochemical knowledge of DNA, and for that I went to Delft to study technical microbiology. There was also a field of study underway there - which is now fully developed - that is, nanotechnology. I studied artificial intelligence in Delft, and in Amsterdam I studied artificial intelligence in so far as it already existed as a field of study at that time; I studied computer science, and also philosophy."

"That's impressive," Els said. "How did you programme all that in those sixteen or eighteen hours that you were awake? You were able to do it all at the same time? Because it didn't take you twelve years - you finished all three studies in the regular six years."

He laughed and said:

"You're either a miracle child or you're not!"

There was a silence.

This theme of 'miracle child' had been the origin of this conversation.

After some time, Els asked:

"If you look back at those six years of study, what important things did you actually learn?"

He pondered; and after a while he said:

"If I have to sum that up, I'd have to say: I have really gained knowledge of the three scientific directions that are going to take over our human development, to help it take wings, to go beyond itself - and those are the sciences of DNA, nanotechnology - that is, the technical possibility of bringing the most complex technology in computer science, for instance, into the smallest technical vehicles, so that eventually chips will be developed, which are becoming ever smaller and smaller, but ever more powerful and ever wiser and ever more independent. And the third is – and that really only surfaced during the course of my studies as a subject then - robot science; and maybe I should say as a fourth, there is the science of thinking itself. I did not find that in philosophy, but in the science of artificial intelligence, where one builds a mind based on investigations of the thinking activity of the human brain. That's where I found the science of thinking the most reliable."

"Yeah, well … " said Els, "of course, that's really impressive! That a human being can master such extensive knowledge!"

"Yes," he said thoughtfully, "but at the same time the realisation arises: how cumbersome the human brain is in action, how clumsy the thought processes actually are when you compare them with the artificial thought processes."

She raised her hands to heaven and exclaimed:

"My dear Raymond! Of course, I know all too well that you adhere to these theories! But how can a miracle child be so incredibly stupid!"

He loved her intensely, perhaps precisely because she outstripped his intelligence with her intuitive 'stupidity'. Sometimes, he thought that her 'stupidity' was the only real intelligence – but, naturally, he always quickly discarded that idea and stuck with his opinion: she doesn't know anything!

Els went on:

"No, I have no arguments to convince you of your prodigal stupidity. I haven't studied enough for that. I have actually studied as well, passed my exams with good grades, got my PhD …and so, apparently, I wasn't that stupid, after all! But in the field where you operate, of this field I indeed know almost nothing. The only things I know are what you tell me about it. And every time we talk about it, I get so incredibly irritated about the stupidity of these ways of thinking that I would like to fly to the moon or something, hoping that only wise creatures live there. For this is truly indescribable!"

He controlled his feelings, and said quietly:

"I think it would be a very good idea if we go into greater depth on this subject when we talk again. For this matters to my life as a scientist - and this is exactly what I would like to entrust to paper, but I don't believe I am able to do so. However, I can tell it all to my dearest Els… who gets immensely irritated by it … !"

They went for a pizza at the Italian restaurant nearby. The restaurant was located in an old butcher's shop with those big old-fashioned refrigerators. The room was still partly tiled and was packed, as packed as it could be, with tables. It was always crowded and the pizza was tasty and authentic Italian.

They got a table in the back and ordered their pizza with a glass of red wine. They were good customers here, coming at least once a week, when they didn't have time or inclination to prepare their own food. When they had toasted each other and had had a sip of wine, Els said, taking an olive:

"Now I'd really like to test your sensibilities ... Do you care if you just get house wine from a jug or the most expensive rich, tasty red wine from the south of Italy?"

He looked at her, shaking his head and said:

"What, are you on the warpath? Why wouldn't I like something that tastes good, more, and something that tastes less, less?"

"For sure ... " she said, "but does it really get through to you that this wine is really good?"

He put his hand on hers and said:

"It gets through to me what an incredibly sweet darling you are! If I didn't have any feelings at all you'd notice, wouldn't you? We've been together almost every day for five years and I don't get the impression that you're unhappy ... "

"No, I'm not," she admitted. "But if I get a glimpse of your inner world like I did this afternoon, I get a feeling of anxiety and then I think: how can you live with that vision of all those neurons and synapses in the brain? These synapses are for this sensation, those synapses for those thoughts - and so on. Whereas, when you take a sip of wine, in one's first impression you know: this wine is really very good Italian wine and not sour vinegar from the supermarket!"

"It really isn't the case that, when I take a sip of wine, the overall impression disintegrates into an almost innumerable amount of synapses to arrive at this sensation. I'm not thinking that, I'm not doing that at all."

"No, but the fact that you *do* do that at other times must have an effect on your whole life, mustn't it?"

"Where are you going with this, Els dear?" He said 'dear', but he was a bit irritated.

"I don't know where I want to go.... Your name is 'Raymond', and maybe you're not aware of it, but the meaning of that name is a very old one: 'a strong protector'. Now I have to be honest with you and say that taking in all the wonderful qualities that you have, that's something that I don't feel at all with you … "

"What don't you feel?"

"That you would be a protector. You're incredibly intelligent, you're also handy, but it seems as if the fighting spirit that a protector needs to have, has somehow passed you by. You are all brains and as far as that works in your fingers, you are indeed capable. But something like a completely impulsive, instinctive, forceful act - that doesn't suit you at all."

"Oh, I don't know? That opportunity hasn't present itself, has it? Suppose someone were to come in here who would want to hurt you, I might indeed turn out to be your protector!"

She laughed and said:

"Hey - do you know I actually believe that, too? But you don't seem to understand what I mean."

"No," he said. "I really don't understand. As far as I am concerned, all actions also originate from impulses, which themselves originate in the brain or in the spinal cord - after all, everything is based on electricity and magnetism; but as a field carrying information, and that, of course, is something very special - that these physical forces are interwoven with knowledge, with informative content. And from that knowing I also might very well be a protector! But what you say, so impulsive, without reflection, without self-awareness … no, I can't see that as an ideal. And if I were to behave like that, I would still know that it is not my highly specialised brain, but the much less developed spinal cord from which I receive such coarse impulses."

The waitress came with the two pizzas and put them cheerfully in front of them.

"So," she said, "maybe this can spice up your serious conversation a little!" and she walked away laughing.

"I think that's a good idea," he said.

He cut his pizza and ate it with relish.

Instead of a dessert they had a cappuccino and remembered the first time they met.

"It was a strange coincidence," he said, "that you and I were in the concert hall, sitting on adjacent chairs, attending the Matthew Passion on Palm Sunday. You were with your sister, I was with two music friends. The two music friends sat on my left and your sister sat on your right, so we were sitting next to each other. I've been going to concerts for decades and when I'm sitting next to a stranger in the row - and that's usually the case - it's not my habit to start a conversation. So it's interesting … When we happened to end up next to each other in the concert hall, a real conversation was struck up … "

"Yes," said Els, "but I always do … I like it when I sit beside someone so 'coincidentally', as you call it, so intimate in fact, that you could, pretty much, sit with your knees touching. When I'm sitting next to someone like that, I always tend to have a conversation. And so I did with you. It's always based on some trivial thing … a bag that gets in the way; or somebody who wants to get past, so we have to get up; the programme that you had - and I didn't. I asked, 'can I see who the musicians performing are?' Yeah, that's what triggered it for us. I thought it was a waste to spend a few euros on a programme like that, which you throw away anyway. But you had bought it, you had it in your hand! I had brought the score, but I didn't know who the performers were, not even the conductor. So I asked you, 'could I take a look in the programme to see exactly who the soloists are here?' You reacted as if you'd been stung by a wasp! You thought it very strange that I just spoke to you - and then asked you for something! But you passed it to me and I checked out the soloists … I knew the soprano very well, so I exclaimed: 'Well, that's special, that she's the soprano here!' You felt addressed anyway and you said something like: 'How special?'- and that's how we got to talking: about soloists who have been at the conservatoire, who have taken Masterclasses in Europe and who finally come to the fore because they're so good, or because they're versatile.

"When the music started I felt your presence beside me very consciously - and maybe I should stop asking whether or not you have deep feelings based on your sensory impressions! Because my first experience of you was that I felt this person next to me who was impressed so deeply by the music that you were sitting beside me, trembling with emotion as it were."

"That's right. I've always had that with Bach's passion music. Always; but that time I had it in particular and I have to tell you, I had the distinct impression that this was because I was sitting next to you."

"I'm actually quite enjoying this…." Els said, as they were sitting across from each other again on Sunday afternoon to continue their 'child prodigy' conversation. "We finished at grammar school, with the music and then went on to the university. How was that time as a student for you?"

"As you would expect, I spent a lot of time on my three areas of study; and I have to say that I gradually developed my own vision, which is very important to me and which I actually value more than my career - although I think a child prodigy should be a bit more successful."

"That's where our conversation began yesterday," said Els, "that you're actually dissatisfied with your career … "

"It's hard to explain. But you have to imagine growing up, while everything around you makes you feel like something extra special. That feeling stayed with me until I graduated. Then I studied for another spell in America on a scholarship. That's when you actually feel how big the scientific world is and how insignificant you are, even if you're gifted. When you feel at home in the scientific environment in America, the feeling of being something special quickly evaporates … "

"Surely it's not the case that all American students are child prodigies?" she said in amazement. "Wouldn't you have been head and shoulders above the average there, too?"

"Yes of course, that's not quite what I mean - it's more that the scientific world is so big there, there's so much in motion, it's moving so fast, there are so many people working in that scientific development, that you feel simultaneously that there's actually no place for you. And at that point when you consider what your future life will look like, then you will see something similar to what it is indeed becoming now!

A very good job, with very good prospects, but in fact - nothing too special."

"But you are special - because you are you! Not because you achieve recognition for your giftedness in the American scientific world?"

"Well, that's not so easy for me. My uniqueness has always been pointed out very strongly - from the outside. It's not that easy for me to feel, within myself, that I have this uniqueness, without longing for external confirmation: in a certain position, in a certain important scientific institute. Apparently, I expected that the whole world would be waiting for me and that I would make a name for myself in the scientific world of information technology, of artificial intelligence and, especially, in the world of hard artificial intelligence."

"You'll have to explain that to me again for the sake of clarity. What's that all about?"

"Okay, then we get to the heart of the matter! We've already talked about it in passing, but it's clear that you don't share my views, my knowledge. It doesn't make much sense to go over this every time, because you don't divert me from my point of view, and I don't divert you from yours either. And to go through life together on and off arguing or debating, I don't like that … "

"Me neither!" she said. "But this is something else. We are now trying - more or less objectively - to write down your life story - as far as it is scientific - and that of course includes your point of view. What I have to say in contrast to that doesn't seem uninteresting in the whole story. Surely we can simply write that down, without feeling that we have to be right?"

"Well, if you can see it that way, I will try to put into words what scientific point of view I have developed in the course of my three studies. I have become very impressed with the pace at which technology is developing. If you look at what one could do in information technology when I started my studies and what one could do when I finished them - there's a world of difference. It's developing so fast that you can hardly help but ask yourself serious questions as it develops into the future. It seems as if not only the speed of development, but also the refinement of the development of information technology is exponential."

"You mean, that when you plot that in a graph, you get a figure that rises slowly at first and then at some point shifts into a gigantic acceleration, so that it seems as if in a short time an increasing, enormous improvement is being achieved … ”

"Exactly, you put it very well. If you look at it from the outside, it may be an interesting whole, of which you could say: okay, it all seems to be developing very quickly, but we'll see where it goes.

"When you are involved in that technological development with your knowledge, then you start to feel, in a way, how fast that development is going and how you, as a human being, are being drawn into it, not to say dragged along with it."

"That doesn't sound too positive," she said.

" Yes, it's like canoeing over waterfalls! But the other way around: in this case it's not going down, but you're still going up and up faster and faster. I understand very well that people who look at this development from the outside, shrug their shoulders about it. We technical scientists, who are part of this development process with our science, are carried along in this stream, whether we are aware of it or not. Within that scientific field there are, of course, also many scientists who are not at all surprised about the speed of development, who also don't feel the need to depict it graphically and then ask themselves: where is it all going? But there is also a very large group of scholars who identify with this development. What actually happens is that, on the one hand, the software of the human body is brought more and more clearly into the picture -"

"Software?!?" she spluttered with a grimace.

"Yes - the whole hereditary disposition in the sequence of DNA molecules and, as we've discussed already, determining the function of every nerve fibre and every synapse in the human brain and thus mapping its functioning. That's what I call 'software'."

"How unattractive! Anyway, we should be remaining objective … "

"Right! That topic's a development in the field of human research itself. Alongside that, there's the development of artificial intelligence. The computer is a machine, in fact a calculator, whatever its name is, it calculates. And this machine's ability to run complicated thought processes by calculation following the example of the human brain, it is that ability that is increasing exponentially. Computers are getting faster and faster, more and more capable, and also smaller. Just look at the mobile phone you have in your hand and which is now recording our conversation.

That small device now has almost more computer skills than those very large PCs from the nineties! I remember seeing an American movie, in which a girl sat on the beach with a device on her lap, without cables. They called it a laptop, a device that you put on your lap. It was the first time I'd seen this miniature wireless computer. Now, the laptop is in fact a kind of giant monstrosity compared to the tablet or the smartphone and it won't be long before that smartphone is a giant monstrosity compared to intelligent chips, which - small as they are in themselves – have an incomparable capacity for information processing: an artificial intelligence that far surpasses the smartphone's ability."

"That means what, exactly?"

"There's another aspect, too. Through technical development we've been able for some time now, to write programs in such a way that the device running them learns from its own programming. We've known about that for a long time from speech recognition. If you want to convert spoken text into written text, you used to have to speak a well-defined piece of text first, and then the device would work in such a way that it could recognise some of the text spoken by that person and convert it into written language. Now we have features like that on our smartphone, and the more you use it, the more accurate and better it gets. That is, the operation corrects itself. Surely, that's really starting to move in the direction of human activity … "

"Excuse me, Raymond, I'd like to see all this objectively, but I can't resist intervening. Because I think it's impossible for you to compare the self-learning principle of a machine with, for example, the self-education of a human being, or the development of certain skills as any human being can. You play the piano beautifully. Are you trying to tell me that your development to the level you are at now, can be seriously compared to what a self-learning computer does when it adjusts its program on the basis of its own experience?"

"Yes, that's precisely what I'm trying to say. And you've just used the word 'experience', yourself! That's exactly the point. Because the opponents of this way of thinking always argue that a machine cannot have experiences. You can say that on the basis of success or failure, without actually feeling it, certain processes adjust, they 'think'. But my experience is something else -"

"Yes, you are right." she said. "I did say the word 'experience' and then I thought, that's not really the right word. I don't believe in a machine having experience. I do witness how your piano playing has become so technically refined and sensitively beautiful with the help of experience. But then again, I have no way of proving that I'm right. I just don't understand how it is possible for you to lump those two very different processes together - there must be something wrong with your discernment, then!"

"Maybe that's so!" he said. "If we want to see this objectively, we'll also have to face that possibility objectively. But first I have to tell you what my point of view is. If you look at the evolution of the species on earth up to 'Man' in a meaningful way then, of course, it cannot be that

over millions of years there has been a grand scheme of development that has continued until the phenomenon of Man - and that from that point onwards evolution would stand still, that there would be no growth, no further development. So the question is, when you look at homo sapiens and you see the further development towards homo sapiens sapiens – "

"What's that?"

"That's the self-conscious human being. That he is not only conscious and can think, but also knows that he thinks, knows that he is there. Then you have to ask yourself: How does evolution continue from homo sapiens sapiens?"

"So far no one has ever wondered," she said, "how evolution will continue. Evolution will continue, and we'll see."

"Oh yes, that's exactly the point!" he said. "I believe - and I'm not the only one who thinks so - that from homo sapiens sapiens there is no further evolution possible other than that humanity takes that evolution into its own hands. When you take that point of view you have to ask yourself: How does evolution proceed now: by taking it into your own hands!"

Els said:

"Do you, as a human being, then see yourself capable of that greatest process of creation - whether or not you consider it a divine process or an evolutionary process based on trial and error - do you, as a human being, see yourself capable of being so brilliant that you could continue that process with your own strength and understanding?"

34

"I think that's the intention, yes."

"'That would then imply, as I see it, that it will be many thousands of years before Man, with his knowledge and control of nature, becomes so far advanced that there may be some possibility that he will transcend his own creation process. If Man's clumsy brain were to lead this process then a few thousand years would seem, to me, to be far too little!"

"Ah - I see it this way: Man invents a technology that is based on the thinking technique of the human brain, but leaves the inconveniences and clumsiness out of it, so that a machine is designed, gradually emerges, which is initially as intelligent as the human brain, but which works more and more efficiently. Not a little more efficiently, but infinitely more efficiently, in an exponential growth. When the point is reached that the expansion of this machine's intelligent power has really increased exponentially, then we arrive at a situation where homo sapiens sapiens is less than this machine."

"But I thought that homo sapiens sapiens was going to take control of further evolution itself? Now you're saying it's a machine that will follow on from the human stage?"

"Yes, but that machine was created by Man, let me say, and when Man succeeds in connecting himself to that machine, fertilizing the potential of human intelligence with the unbridled technological growth of the use of artificial intelligence, then a new kind of Man emerges, enriching himself with that artificial intelligence."

"How is that clumsy human brain of homo sapiens sapiens supposed to keep up with that frenzied technological development of artificial intelligence? Won't that completely dominate you, then?"

"No, if we succeed in connecting this rapidly developing intelligence, which is the artificial one, with our own possibilities of thinking, then we will actually have the feeling that it is we ourselves who are thinking, when that technical intelligence becomes active in us".

"But then - there's something else you have to take into account," she said. "And that is, that there also have to be people who want this. I remember reading a prediction from the beginning of the 21st century, that at the end of the first decade or so - that is, around 2010 - everybody would be walking around wearing a certain type of glasses - in a virtual world, being intelligent! We're writing 2019 and I don't see them, these people with the glasses. Maybe they put on such glasses to watch TV in 3D, but a lot of people simply don't feel the need for them, either. So, the question is: whether what you then envisage as a possibility for humans - to transcend human evolution through a kind of 'technological explosion' I'd say - it's a question of whether you can find people who want to participate in that."

"I know people well enough, don't I? I got to know them in America, went to lectures there, talked to a lot of people. Of course, most people don't even think about it. But isn't that precisely the hallmark of evolution: that the most progressive, the most perfected of the species are making or showing the transition to a new species?"

Els leaned back and raised her hands in supplication.

"Oh, boy, Raymond! This is really terrible! What arrogance … I'm just as non-religious as you are. I don't believe in God or Commandments, really. But listening to your vision I really wish there was indeed a God, who at some point would pick up a broom, sweep you all into a pile and wipe you all off the face of the earth and say: 'Well this is no use to us, go to Hell, you arrogant human beings'!"

Raymond laughed and said:

"Maybe I'm not actually as non-religious as you? I'm still a long way from the question: Where is the origin of this whole process? Is it really in physics, chemistry, in a miraculous process of development that regulates itself, in which the successful forms are preserved and the less successful ones are rejected? Or is there, after all, a super being behind all these processes - who thinks in the way I imagine that artificial intelligence will finally think - who devised this whole thing, and is now trying it out?"

"What a beautiful religious representation that is!" she said. "God sitting at the keyboard with headphones and virtual glasses on: 'Let's just try, a little bit of this - doesn't work! Next try, a bit of that - oh look, what's created now! I like that, let's develop that further…' "

" You are not being serious, and certainly not objective!" He was a bit irritated by now."

" 'Try to stay objective here!' This is terrible … What a sweet man you are, and how intelligent and artistic … But when you start expressing these thoughts, I get an image - well, I won't say it, but it's not beautiful."

"But you do know that's how I think, don't you?"

" Yes, but I just can't believe that you really believe that, through and through. I just can't! If you did, you'd be a robot, a guy with a brilliant intelligence, but absolutely no sensitivity. And you are not like that, you are nice – and so why can't that kindness within you convince you that what you think is not actually true? I wish I could explain it to you, but I don't have the arguments."

She said abruptly:

"Okay - let's go on."

"Not only are we looking for a way to embody this artificial intelligence in carriers so small that you can insert them into the human body, we are also striving for an ever-increasing speed of transmission of information. So far, the limit seems to be the speed of light, but when the growth of the speed increases as exponentially as it seems to be doing now, then there comes a moment when that speed outstrips the speed of light. Then it would become possible to fill the entire cosmos with meaningful coherent artificial intelligence. Up until now, that coverage does not really extend beyond the earth's immediate environment. But there could come a time when the cloud of information could spread out over the whole cosmos at a greater speed than light can, and even radiate through the black holes to outside cosmic areas - that is to say, areas we cannot know yet."

"Interesting," Els said calmly. He looked at her attentively, but he didn't detect any sense of mockery. Apparently, she was beginning to see that there was a grain of truth - and also of possibility - in his view …

"But," started Els, "Surely you once read Roger Penrose's book, The Emperor's New Mind?"

"Yes," he said, "a superficially popular booklet … "

"Well, booklet … I had quite a bit of trouble reading it through, anyway. But it's interesting, and it describes very clearly that while a computer can solve the most complicated problems, the very simple everyday ones are almost insurmountable for it?"

"That was in the nineties," he said. "In the meantime, such problems have long since been overcome."

"Well, I suppose so," she said, not really believing it. "I remember that it describes an experiment in which the computer is asked whether or not a hamburger will be eaten on the basis of a short story about eating a hamburger. A man goes into a restaurant and orders a hamburger. He gets the hamburger, doesn't like it and leaves without paying the bill. That's one story; and the other story is: a man goes into a restaurant and orders a hamburger. He likes the hamburger, pays the bill and leaves. The question was, if I remember correctly: in which of the cases did the man eat the hamburger? It turned out to be rather difficult for the computer to determine from the data that in one case the man had left the hamburger, and in the other he had eaten the hamburger! There was also mention of an experiment by John Searle in a Chinese room: this showed that although he does not know Chinese, he can still use Chinese characters to know what is written, as long as he has the right algorithm at his disposal. He proved that without knowing the language, he could still read it. I don't remember exactly, but it was something like that. It's also been said that the number of calculation steps the computer has to get through to answer such a simple question about eating the hamburger is gigantic - while a person, hearing such a story, immediately knows the answer to the question."

It looked as if Raymond had been thrown off balance for a moment, but he recovered quickly and replied:

"Those, of course, are the bumps we have to accept. After all, the human brain is also working with non-scientific everyday facts, which are indeed more difficult to program than the most complicated mathematical task."

"Isn't that why," said Els, "because people immediately form images in such stories? You see it in your mind's eye - and the computer can't do that, it calculates away monotonously and eventually comes up with an answer. As far as I'm concerned, it's more or less a matter of good luck whether it's right. After all, it has a fifty percent chance of giving the right answer, even though it doesn't understand what it's all about!"

"What you're raising now is the question of consciousness. That is indeed a difficult question. Scientifically speaking, the phenomenon of consciousness remains a difficult subject. And you are right when you say that it is indeed a question whether a machine that knows how to solve a complex problem with a calculation method, is aware of this whole process."

"I don't think so!" Els said immediately.

"That's a subjective reaction! We in science are intensively concerned with the question of whether being able to carry out a thought process doesn't at the same time mean that there is consciousness as well."

Els took a deep breath and said:

"I am glad that I have a 'subject' in my thinking; and that I can spontaneously realize the sheer impossibility of what you are trying so hard to find out scientifically: whether a machine thinking process necessarily goes hand in hand with consciousness! What nonsense! You know that spontaneously, don't you, that it doesn't? When you imagine how such a device works, guided entirely by the algorithms you have put into it, then that device runs blindly through those processes. It is of course super-objective, it has no sense of truth or falsehood, of correctness or inaccuracy, but simply rushes like a train from one station to another, ruthless and certainly not with consciousness! That would be the same as if I were to say that my washing machine, because it is computer-controlled, would know what it is doing - that it knows when it's doing white washing at 60 degrees. It does it because I set it up. That it'd be conscious of that, too? Raymond, I'm sorry, but that's not a question of any substance, is it?"

There was a silence. How was he supposed to answer that? Actually, in a way, he felt they were at checkmate, even though he was completely convinced she wasn't right. Just as she thought she saw that a machine that thinks has no consciousness, so he thought he saw that a machine that thinks has to have consciousness.

"Have you never played with model trains before?" she asked.

He laughed and said:

"What's that got to do with it?!"

"A lot!" she said. "This whole process of thinking machines reminds me very much of a train marshalling yard, where the points are set in a certain way so that the train has no choice but to travel a certain route along those points. I think, roughly, that is a paradigm for those thinking machines of yours. Of course, they are infinitely small and multi-branched, but the basic principle always remains: do you go left, or do you go right? or do you go straight on? When you have established that in advance, you cannot, when you come to a junction, think: would I go straight ahead, or would I turn left, or would I turn right? Whatever is pre-programmed, that's what you have to do, so the thinking simply runs as though it cannot be done in any other way. But there's no way to compare that to a typically human trait, is there?"

Again, it fell silent. Raymond said:

"You can see it's fine in itself, but what you're overlooking is the self-learning activity that we, as programmers, can also build into an algorithm."

"But then that process, which is itself self-learning, ends according to certain patterns that you have put in it first, right? Isn't that something completely different from thinking, at a certain moment, something that is absolutely original - and which you know is original?"

"According to us, that is just an illusion, and the thinking process with biological information ends just as automatically as it does with a self-learning computer; that these things you are saying to me right now are themselves based on your biological information."

"That would mean," she said, "that you can never convince me of your vision."

"That depends," he said, "to what extent your biological predisposition is such that this self-learning element, which would allow you to rise above your organic state, can be set in motion in you."

"No freedom, then," she said, becoming somewhat gloomy.

"I can tell myself that 'I am an original thinking and creating human being', but in fact there is an algorithm hidden in my organization that makes me think and do exactly what is prescribed in it and that could be transcended if I could be given the opportunity to enrich and refine my biological organic predisposition with the help of artificial intelligence. And this will not be located outside of you, as it is now in the PC or in a laptop or smartphone, but which is introduced into your organism, so that you can unite the possibilities of that higher-level algorithm with the algorithm that you already have from your biological predisposition."

"I really think it's a very interesting train of thought," said Els. "And, indeed, it's a wonderful theme for science fiction literature as well, which of course it already is. But that there could be a human being who believes all that, a flesh-and-blood human being, with a heart - I find that incomprehensible…. and that that is you," she added, "I find that terrible!"

He became a little anxious and thought: here's hoping this biographical experiment doesn't lead to a separation of minds, because Els is now gaining insight into my deepest convictions and she has absolutely no suitable mode of perception for it … Still, he also sensed a very small hint of doubt about his own vision, which was what had prompted this … There was something in her reasoning that called the matter into question - and he didn't know exactly what it was. It seemed as if he, likewise, didn't have a mode of perception for it …

"But go on," she said. "It's all very interesting, what you are describing. What is this theory based on? What's its origin?"

"All right, but let me say at the outset," he said, "that I don't see it as a theory, but as a realistic vision of the future. The origin is longer ago than you'd think. In 1965, one of the founders of the large company Intel – the company that manufactures computer chips - began a study on the speed of technological development. His name is Gordon Moore. On the basis of that study he came up with a law, namely: that the number of transistors in an integrated circuit doubles every year. That generates an exponential curve, when you plot that on a graph. It is based on this assumption that, in the end, technological development will accelerate to such an extent that it will not only exceed the capacity of the human brain but will leave it far, far behind as it grows exponentially."

Els said:

"But it's not just about the number of transistors in a circuit, is it?"

"Some time after that, he adjusted that vision and estimated the doubling to every two years. No, it's not just about those transistors, it also means that, proportionally, a reduction in the size of the device is possible - which we can see in the smartphone – which is actually a computer - or even in the smartwatch. When you add nanotechnology to that, you see, as I said, a possibility in the not too distant future to build an entire computer on a chip the size of a blood cell."

"Has his prediction come true?" Els asked.

"Well, to be honest, Moore himself said in 2005 that the growth was reaching a limit and that there are physical barriers to be overcome - and that it is not as simple as that."

"I always think," said Els, "that when forecasting the future, it's better to look at what doesn't turn out than what does. What does turn out correctly feeds the vision, but what doesn't turn out is often forgotten. You remember, in 2012 the world was to end on 12 – 12? That was because of a certain era in the Mayan calendar. Well, it didn't perish, and meanwhile people are going on living and not pulling their hair out because they were stupid enough to believe it!"

"I don't think there's any risk that this vision isn't going to come true. Physical barriers? We have achieved such far-reaching results in nanotechnology that we'd expect the whole riddle of matter to be solved in such a way that it will be possible to synthesize any substance you want."

"Even gold?" she enquired.

"Gold too! If we master the technique of making the atoms themselves synthetic using nanotechnology, it will be possible to make any existing element'.

"Modern alchemy," she said.

"Yes, but then stripped of all magical speculation."

"You also studied philosophy. Did you come across any thinkers in that field whose worldview can underpin such a vision of the future?"

"Yes." He said, "You asked about the origin of this vision. It was during the period after the Second World War and at that time there was a lot going on with regard to a vision that in the new century - the one, therefore, in which we are now living - a total change of the human race would occur. A new evolutionary step. It's not just artificial intelligence that has led up to it. In philosophy you also find a thinker who builds his prophecy on the development of the technical possibilities of communication."

"Who is that, then?"

"Pierre Teilhard de Chardin."

"And you saw something in that prophecy?"

"I still see a great deal in it."

"But he was a Jesuit!"

Raymond laughed, and observed:

"You really know everything! Yes, he was a Jesuit."

"And as I recall," she said, "his vision of the future is one that is deeply religious. That doesn't fit in at all with your own vision, does it?!"

42

"You can't just say that," he said. "Of course, we really do wonder what the moral consequences will be of this step in the evolution of the universe. And we also wonder if this evolution has any, let's say, spiritual meaning."

"You don't believe in any of that, do you?" Els said in amazement.

"I don't believe in that, not so directly ... " he said, "but I want to consider it. And it's plausible in itself, even if you only take in what this thinker has written, that a new step in evolution is approaching. That's what the 'singularitarians' say. We are faced with a shock in evolution, in which the crown of creation - Man - will surpass itself and create a new species, which through trans-human development will finally lead to a post-human living species. This is exactly what this Pierre Teilhard de Chardin also describes, but with him this is supported by a profound sense of morality: 'Global communion until mankind as a whole is one organism.' He mentions the origin - or the end point - which everything gravitates toward, but which derives its impulses from an originally divine act, one could say, in a great encompassing cosmic consciousness, to which Man will evolve, but which is already present without Man. He gives this a name drawn from the Apocalypse in the Bible: 'the Omega Point.' "

"That's terrifying ... But why do I feel all the time that there's some truth in it, but it doesn't get to the truth? That it's off balance in its line of reasoning? And yet I would have absolutely no idea where to find any arguments to support my impression."

"Probably you are afraid of this turbulent renewal."

"I don't believe that," she said. "I don't feel fear, but I do feel it's not right. Just as you can experience with a patient who comes into the consulting room with a completely innocent symptom, and then you get the feeling: something's not right, be wary, there's something completely different about this than the symptoms would have you believe!"

"Yes," he said, " you are really very good at that, at sensing danger in a person's life."

"Exactly," she said, "that's how I feel danger here, too, in a way. But I've been trained to think, apart from all the rational thoughts, that it's alright to have intuitions on whatever it might be. The patient who comes in with inconspicuous symptoms, you have to dare to refer him on and maybe save a life. In what we are discussing now, I have exactly the same feeling. I know it's something else, but I'm not trained to see how. I'm telling you: it's not right, you're on the wrong track with your vision!"

Again, he got that strange feeling that she might be right. It was as if there was a crack in the reinforced concrete, as if there were signs of fatigue in the construction.

"You're far too good - I mean, kind, sweet, gentle, to be carrying in your head such a desolate vision of the future, as colourless as the brain itself … "

"I don't think it's desolate at all, I think it's extraordinarily exciting and I'm looking forward to the next developments."

"But you also read the newspaper, don't you? You read about the other side of this technical development, don't you? Namely, that in the long run there will no longer be a corner of the earth in which you can hide; that everything you think, what you feel, what you do, will be public? And when you are injected with a computer on a chip the size of a cell … Surely you have to see that you then carry inside you a program created by someone who has nothing to do with you? In this way mankind can be transformed into a stupid herd of people, who don't know what original thinking is anymore and who let themselves glide along in a virtual reality. Because you haven't talked about any of that yet. What would our environment look like in that post-human era?"

"That will be entirely in your own hands. Just as you are able now, if you want to see a classic temple, travel to Greece, or maybe see a Buddhist temple, for example, travel to Thailand; you'll be able simply to create that around you, so that you can be exactly where you want to be."

"In images," she said.

'Not really in images, they'll be indistinguishable from the real thing. You'll feel the wind through your hair, smell the scent of the pine trees, and so on. Exactly as it is where you imagine you are … "

"Oh my God!" she said, "this is getting worse! Will there still be a way to get into the non-virtual reality?"

"That's the question," he said. "The question is: would you still want to do that? To step into that shabby and barren contrast that will be 'reality', while you can indulge in anything you want in virtual reality."

"Linguistically speaking, you cannot justify what you are saying now: 'virtual reality'! But how should I imagine that, how can a human being be satisfied with a mimicked nature?"

"If you, as a child, are used to this from the cradle, then you will not be bothered by it."

"This reminds me," said Els, "of a novel I once read - I believe it was by a Danish writer. The title was, 'A Man in the Madhouse'."[1]

"Anker Larsen."

"Right! At the end of the book it turns out that the man who's in the madhouse because he's crazy, is actually the only one who still has a healthy psychic human nature - that's why he's locked up in a madhouse! Something like that seems to be happening here. And what about death - because I don't think we've reached the point where death has been conquered through technical development - have we?"

"I'm not so sure about that. If your mind is as miraculous as you think it is - as your feelings are - if that could be expressed in an algorithm…. then you would be immortal."

"Except that I wouldn't know I was there … " she said. "Remember that old saying, 'If I was a king and I didn't know, I wouldn't be a king'."

"Meister Eckhart. Of course, you'll know you're there. Your very own specific way of thinking and feeling will evoke your very own specific nature of consciousness."

"Well … " she said, "as far as I'm concerned, that's enough for today. Maybe you could play some Bach for me? So I can feel that you're a real human being?"

He sighed deeply and for a moment felt a tinge of fear rising within him again, at the risk of losing her to this future vision. He got up and went to the grand piano and played four prelude and fugue pieces by Johann Sebastian Bach. When he had finished, he got up and gave her a hug.

"Magnificent," she said, "really magnificent. Bach's compositions are truly incomparable."

"Except," he said, "to artificial intelligence. One of those four was a synthetic Bach prelude and fugue, composed according to the pattern of Bach's compositions."

She stood back from him and scrutinised him. How much she loved this man!

---

[1] '1941 A Man in the Madhouse' (re-issued in 2006 under the title: 'Olsen's Folly')

She said:

"Raymond, I heard that: it was the fourth."

He looked at her in bewilderment and said:

"Why, the fourth?"

"The fourth prelude and fugue you played wasn't Bach's. Do you think, as a lover of Bach, one wouldn't notice that? That one wouldn't hear that it's a mindless copy of his creations, that it's like an artful bouquet of plastic flowers? Did you really think I wouldn't hear that?"

In the course of the week there was neither time nor energy to continue these conversations. They both had busy jobs and, in the evening after work, when they had eaten and tidied everything up, they watched some television or they sat down with a glass of wine and talked about superficial things, about the events of the day. The big theme had to wait until the next weekend. Seen from the outside everything had remained the same as before, but inside there was a big difference. With Raymond there was a kind of unease, a feeling of insecurity, as to whether Els could continue to love a man with such strange views as his. Even though she remained composed, he saw how his ideas about the future of Man affected her. He couldn't imagine a life without Els at all, and he did his utmost to show his love in everyday little things.

Els could not sleep anymore. She lay awake every night for hours, fighting with the feelings and thoughts that the conversations had stirred in her. Sometimes in half sleep she could suddenly be startled by the thought that there was no human next to her at all, but that beneath that warm beloved skin and muscle lay, in fact, the iron rods of a robot, with joints like cogwheels and a head like a computer. Raymond didn't notice anything of her nightly fears.

Sometimes, in the light of the clear moon, she lay watching him while he was sleeping quietly. She looked at his beloved head with the hair thinning slightly, she heard his calm breathing, felt his radiating warmth. She thought: if his consciousness is not there, then he is innocent, but as soon as he wakes up and his brain starts spinning again, those idiotic thoughts arise in him; which she couldn't really live with.

In her work she had to deal on a daily basis with people of flesh and blood who came to the doctor because they were troubled by something. It didn't occur to her to think of a post-human species in whom the phenomenon of disease would probably have been overcome, because people would have become technologically enriched devices. But in contrast, she was often alarmed by the reports in professional literature about the increasing influence of the computer in research, diag-

47

nosis and prognosis. What used to be entirely in the intuitive power of the doctor, was now calculated by a machine; for example, the degree of probability that someone would eventually develop dementia on the basis of the available DNA. More and more such things could be calculated according to current standards. She was horrified by this, and when she talked about it with certain colleagues, she felt that she was seen as a kind of old-fashioned human being who was not keeping up with modern times – although she was of course still young enough herself … . On the other hand, there were also many colleagues who agreed with her, but who usually didn't carry their thoughts to the point where they could actually imagine what the future of the doctor would be. In that sense, she did find in her profession the omens of what Raymond had pictured for her as an extreme consequence of technological development. But she saw it more as something that mankind should fight with all its might rather than as an exciting, interesting or desirable ideal. Now she had discovered that Raymond did indeed have such developments in mind as an ideal, and as a result there was a gulf between them.

When he slept next to her like that, he had a beating heart and calm breathing, he was warm, he was a human being, a biological living and mortal phenomenon.

She had no thoughts about life before birth or after death, she was hardly even aware of them. But in life between birth and death she felt Man as a mysterious, unfathomable miracle. And for her, the geography of the brain was not at all indicative of this miraculous phenomenon of Man.

So, she lay there awake, next to him, sometimes fearful, sometimes confident. Her mind was confused by the multiplicity of information he had given her, the value he attached to it that it might have real implications for the future. All she could do was be fearful; all he could do was pursue the fruits of his vision.

She searched his bookcase and found a book about the Singularity by a certain Ray Kurzweil. She also took the books of Teilhard de Chardin off the shelf and began to read. When she couldn't sleep at night she would get up and read for a few hours. Before they talked again over the weekend, she wanted to be better informed about this vision of the future – from one perspective grotesque, but from another, a real possibility.

She wondered why she actually loved this man so much. After meeting each other on that occasion in the concert hall, they had immediately taken out their diaries to make another date, and that was how it had always been. Every meeting they got out their diaries, and made a new appointment. For both of them there was a longing for the next meeting.

He wasn't a really handsome boy, nor was he ugly, but he was interesting. You felt his ability to understand and his artistic talent, you felt that he was a great man and he was also very nice, had a lot of patience, could listen well. You felt that he not only had an open ear, but that he really understood what you were saying. And so she fell in love with his ability to understand. His whole outer appearance seemed to be a kind of visible power of understanding. As she now put it into words for herself, it rekindled the fire of love in her again. But all the more painful was the contrast with his idiotic scientific vision of the future.

She really couldn't understand how a man with such artistic powers of comprehension could lose himself in images of a man who would reduce himself by conjoining himself to a calculator. Because a computer remains a calculator, after all. And how could it be that a right-minded person did not realize innately that the brain has capacities other than basic arithmetic? That a computer functions with programs where everything is converted into arithmetic, does not mean that as an example of a thinking-machine - namely the human being - this also is the case. She could faultlessly distinguish that synthetic Bach piece of music in the middle of the real Bach music. That did not come about by calculation, that is not in fact what could have happened. Synthetic music was composed on the basis of certain patterns found in the original composer's work. She could still imagine that. But apparently, in comparison with many of his contemporaries, it was specific to Bach that he had measures in his music that did not meet any pattern at all. She had an organ of perception, which was aware of that. And in the synthetic Bach piece she had recognized merely patterns, and thought: If I knew that pattern through and through, I would be able to write new Bach music into infinity - and then no part of it would be interesting. She thought of a remark by Carl Maria von Weber who had attended Beethoven's seventh symphony and had said, as a kind of review, that Beethoven had really 'lost his mind'. It was precisely that symphony, whose second movement can completely enrapture you with its beauty, which was dismissed by the bourgeois composer as insane. That quality in music could never be matched by a computer.

She also thought of the book by Roger Penrose, who, in his explanations, went to great lengths to demonstrate that the action of the human brain cannot be captured in an algorithm. For her, this was also immediately logical, without need of proof. How could it be that her dearest, insightful partner apparently did not understand this?

Sometimes she thought: I will jump on a plane to Nepal or New Zealand or New Guinea - and I will live among the Papuans to avoid this miserable nonsense! But she wasn't born for that. She was a modern woman and she loved Raymond and she felt a kind of sacred mission awakening in herself to help this man out of his scientific dream …

On Saturday afternoon they sat down opposite each other again, the iPhone on the table between them to record the conversation. He took the initiative and said:

"I've had some concerns about our relationship this past week … Last weekend I shared with you my worldview and vision of the future and, of course, I noticed very clearly that you reject it, even more than that, you think it's a horrific vision. Is it okay that I share these things so openly with you? Wouldn't it be better if I just kept these things to myself and didn't burden you with them?"

"Then," she said, "you'd force me to stick my head in the sand. It's better that I know what's going on with you."

"But," he said, "I'm afraid it will eventually lead to a rift between us."

"No way!" she said. "I love you far too much for that, and I can't imagine living a life without you while we're on this earth. If death were to force us to break up, that would be something else! But I don't believe I would ever abandon you, even if I found out that not only you do think bad things, but you also do them."

He gazed ahead, thoughtfully.

"Do you really think the things I think are bad?"

"Yes," she said.

"Why?"

"Because there's a very great error underlying it that I can't put my finger on. I'd have to become a classmate of yours to find the arguments to

50

convince you that your vision is not right … It has taken such a firm hold on you that I don't feel able to change it. And, of course, I've suffered from that over this past week. I just wish you'd never read and study and think things like that. In the hours that I couldn't sleep at night I read part of that book that you know well….by Ray Kurzweil, on singularity. I think it's a collection of his hobbyhorses. If you keep on reading through it, you start to see that it's still the same hobbyhorse he's making quite a display of. I have often read books by American authors who have become completely lost in a certain vision and then seem to exhibit some kind of narrowing of consciousness, which makes it impossible for them to perceive and think rationally for the rest of their existence.

"Of course, what he writes is very interesting and, apparently, many of his predictions for the future have come true. But as I said, you'd be better to look at what doesn't come true. And I think there's also a very big part of his show that hasn't come true. When I'm reading it, I feel that he gets stuck in the electrical circuits of the brain and the computer, and that he no longer perceives the flesh and blood and the other organs of the human body …"

Raymond interrupted her and said:

"But he does! For example, he lives very healthily because he knows very well that he has to keep his physical body as young and vital as possible, in order to be able to experience the realisation of his vision of the future, and to transform it into a kind of immortality!"

"Look!" Els said, "This is just what I mean! That's nonsense! Of course, technology is slowly touching on life, too. I understand that the miraculous encoding of DNA is now also being used in computers. It's not yet clear to me if this is synthetic DNA, or if it's borrowed from viral material. But the coding given in the basic pattern of DNA provides an almost infinite number of possibilities to reach certain solutions to problems. I understand that - so in that sense the technology is touching on life. But I don't get the impression that technology actually knows what life is. That life itself can be awakened - I don't see anything of that; and what I also don't see is what knowledge exists about what consciousness is, exactly. What I do see, however, is a growing knowledge of how the thought processes in the brain proceed. But how it is possible, too, for a human being to understand this, is still unknown, I believe."

"That depends on what you want to call consciousness. If you assume that thinking as it works in the brain also provides consciousness by the nature of that process, then you have solved the problem."

"Yes," she said, "theoretically, you have: but is it actually true? How would you like to prove that by experiment?"

"We are indeed at the very beginning … " he admitted. "But with the knowledge of how the brain works, it is possible using technology to artificially repair certain processes that have been interrupted by damage. Whoever receives this therapy has an awareness of this."

"That proves nothing at all," she said, "for the one who receives the therapy is already a being with consciousness! The whole DNA technology still depends on the use of microorganisms that carry this DNA, multiply it, copy it and so on. On its own, life cannot be awakened, as I see it."

"That's a matter of time - and given the exponential growth of development, that time won't be too long."

"I find," she said, "that there, you are losing contact with reality. And as a scientist, you shouldn't do that!"

He began to get a little irritated. What does she actually think she knows?

"You are starting to get annoyed … " she said. "I can understand that, because I don't know anything, but I do work daily with living people who have anomalies in their life processes. And whether they rely on DNA patterns or not, I see that life is something that works almost essentially in the human body. You only really perceive that when you see someone dying or when you see someone who has just died. It's a great omission that your artificial intelligence scientists are not obliged to see dying people and people who have just died, while studying."

"You mean, because it makes the brain silent?"

"Yes, and you would see - I can't imagine that you wouldn't see this - you would see that not only does the brain become silent and the heart becomes silent and the breathing stops - but you would see that something is changing, which is irreversible. You could almost say: life is something that subsists with the body as long as it lives and that, as it were, departs when death arrives."

Raymond was quiet; after a while, he said:

"What's that supposed to mean?"

52

"That this should exhort you to humility. That you have no idea what life really is, and that you have no idea at all, how you can awaken life. If you could grow a computer on the basis of virus-DNA that is alive, then you might be able to handle an already living organism. But you'd still have to know that you needed the virus to derive life from it – and, that you're not able to add life to a device or bring it to life yourself."

"You're right about that," he said, "but I don't see why it's so important. The point is, after all, that we can develop machines that have a way of thinking that is as alive as human thought and that, because of the enormous increase in its possibilities, will finally reach a stage in which this equals human thought, only then to rapidly transcend these possibilities."

"I'm not saying I'm sure that it is not possible. It may be possible to do that; but that you see that as desirable and that you can say that the thinking that then emerges surpasses human thinking - I find that so nonsensical, it makes me despair! I really don't understand how you can be so short-sighted - that you don't experience within yourself what a richness human thought has over the calculation of a computer, even though it is so intelligent through self-learning."

They sat silently together for a while. Then Els resumed her argument:

"Then I also read a number of essays by Pierre Teilhard de Chardin. I can imagine how the Catholic Church banned them! But I can also imagine that once these writings were published, they were sold in their millions, because there is something very sympathetic and attractive about them, too. He sees technical development and the development of the media encompassing the whole world as an opportunity for fraternisation in mankind, and he wants to see it in such a way that this eventually leads to a change, to a total mutual sympathy amongst everyone; in such a way that it is no longer possible to feel any antipathy towards your fellow human. You will truly love your fellow man, your neighbour, as you normally love only yourself - and perhaps even more. He argues that in doing so, the personality will be preserved and even strengthened, because it will feel even stronger as a result of that enormous sympathy. This sympathy movement would then bring about a community formation all over the world, so powerful, so strong, that mankind would become an organism. In a way, that's what we all long for. You know, the feeling when you sing in a choir and all the singers have only one common aspiration and that is to perform the music as well and as beautifully as possible. In this way, mankind would become a choir with the sole purpose of fulfilling mankind's character as well and as beautifully as possible, so that it approaches a point to which it feels attracted - and that it really does itself approach. That is the Omega point, which he then presents in such a way that the mankind of brotherly love, which knows only sympathy, becomes the body in its totality for the spirit of the Omega point - and that is Christ. Although we are not Christian - neither you nor me - we do love Bach's passion music and experience in that music every year what John and Matthew wrote about it in the Bible. Apparently, this is not without effect, because when reading about this Christian technological vision, I was really touched. Much more touched than by Kurzweil's display of his hobbyhorses."

"You say it very beautifully, Els, really."

"I think it's very beautiful too, although I have an immediate experience that it can't be like that. What I do think is that mankind could end up becoming the body of Christ, or the meaning of the earth, or something that could lead to fraternisation. But that this has something to do with technology? I can still imagine that a very special technique could be developed that has to do with the point Omega. But that computer technology as we now have it, either directly, or through an exponential growth as I understand it, would lead to such a fraternisation of mankind - that seems impossible to me."

Raymond said:

"It's clear. I will try again tomorrow to present my vision to you in such a way that I take into account your objections from today. Not to convince you, because I don't believe that would work, but maybe I can remove some of your discomfort."

"I hope so … ' said Els. "Really, Raymond, I do hope so."

They walked hand in hand to the pizzeria. It was very busy on this Saturday evening, the owner had to offer her regrets that she did not have a table at her disposal.

"But you know," she said, "if you go around the block now, don't make it too small, and you come back here, I'll have a table for you."

"All right," he said. "How big does the block have to be?"

"I'd say," she said, "you walk into Van Breestraat as far as Emmastraat and then back through Johannes Verhulst. By that time, I'll have it ready here."

And so the walk was extended. They both felt uncomfortable. He, because he was worried; she, because she couldn't grasp it all, that he could warm to this vision.

So they had nothing to say to each other. But after walking in silence for a few hundred meters, he spoke his mind:

"You know, Els … " he said, "maybe I'm sensing some seeds of doubt about this vision I have for the world. You seem to me to be the only one who's capable of making me doubt. But the question is whether I want to. And I feel very clearly that that's just not palatable for you. You don't want to see me like this. You look at my heart and you love my mind as long as it's tied into my heart. When it comes to thinking in itself, you don't want to come with me anymore. And I'm really wondering, will our relationship last?"

She squeezed his hand and said:

"Surely the fact that we can talk about this so openly indicates the value of our relationship? But you're right, I find it hard to accept that you use your giftedness to think only with your frontal lobes and simply ignore the connection to your heart - where, as far as I'm concerned, the truth resides.

"Of course, it is interesting, that vision of yours. On the one hand, I think the future perspective is over-exaggerated. Yet you can also see how artificial intelligence is advancing, it's the same in my own profession. But I believe that I can see the trend being rather more towards the enslaving of mankind by mapping every personality than towards a liberation by a liberating intelligence. You see such a thing in front of you as if the intelligence is no longer limited by the boundaries of the physical. I think there is something completely different in intention, as far as one can speak of intention … ”

"Then we come to the world of conspiracy theories."

"I don't know what world we'll be in. I don't know if there's a Dr. No somewhere who' s turning the knobs, or if it's mankind as a whole itself that is so tempted by the desire for domination and power to let the genie out of the bottle who can't be put back in."

" Genie out of the bottle?" he asked.

"Yes! What's missing from your upbringing is playing with electric trains and listening to Grimm's fairy tales! That's why you don't have such moral images at your disposal that stay with you all your life. How can you imagine that humanity, striving for money and power, will make a moral use of any evolutionary leap to artificial intelligence hooked into the human being?"

"That has to be worked on," he said.

"It certainly has to be worked on! But I'm hearing nothing about that, except for Teilhard de Chardin, who has an optimistic view of the development of mankind. By the way, I think that, with his faith in the future, he got lost in his frontal lobes."

"What's that supposed to mean?"

"I mean, it's completely abstract to say that a time will come when all antipathy and evil will disappear from mankind … Why would that happen if people individually, one by one, don't aspire to that? I can't picture that."

By this time, they were walking through the Johannes Verhulststraat back to the restaurant.

"I think I really do understand where your objections lie, and I respect them too. I'm just afraid that I won't be allowed to hold on to my vision of the future if I want to stay with you."

"Of course, you can think what you want!" she said, "and you can see what you want, too. I've already told you, I won't leave you for that reason. But I will suffer and I will do my best to help you out of this dream. Only I sense my powerlessness in this, because I reason in a completely different way than you, and I have the feeling that with my way of reasoning I am not reaching your way of thinking."

He wrapped an arm around her and pulled her towards him and said:

"Oh yes, you do reach me! I also notice in certain points of your argument that you touch on something I have to take seriously. It's not so much the articulated details, but it's more the form of your reasoning."

"That's my heart," she said.

"I don't know, I have no idea. But I do experience something of a form of truth in your thinking that cannot be congruent with my own. If only I could think that it doesn't matter, I'd be done with it in no time. But there are moments sometimes when I do experience that form and I feel a crack in my mental framework."

"The point is," she said, "that this vision of the future is always traced back to Moore's well-known law - that's what I mean by the hobbyhorse - and while Moore himself had already indicated in 2005 that his law had reached a limit, the rest of the world continues to highlight it and carries on thinking about it. This gives rise to the idea of singularity that Kurzweil already predicts will occur during the course of this century. By the way, I find it ridiculous that this man's name is Kurzweil. Because if you wanted to make up a mocking nickname for all those people with a gifted mind, you would choose a name for the opposite of boredom: a nerd never gets bored - "

"So?" he said.

"So? You know the German word for tedium, don't you? Langweilen. So, what would you call a nerd like that? Kurzweil … "

He was laughing.

"Yeah, that's kind of weird. You think he's not taking into account a certain law in the universe?"

"It seems to me there is rhythm in the universe, too, and there is something like tedium, when things cannot continue to develop. You even see in the Bible - I remember that from school - that God created the world, that he accomplished it in six days, but that he rested on the seventh day? That's kind of a reflection on the fact that what he'd made was right."

"That's the Bible, dear darling!"

"Yet a kind of primal image of creation it seems to me. Possibly simply depicted, yet with a primal rhythm … "

By now they were standing in front of the restaurant and actually wanted to carry on talking. But having reached the goal of their walk, they went inside, where indeed an empty table was waiting for them …

They resumed the conversation on Sunday afternoon.

"Let me unfold my vision for you once again and take your objections into account."

"If you can … " she smiled.

"I can at least try! If you don't want to see Moore's law as a permanent principle, then when you look at the development of the computer, of computer science, of artificial intelligence, of robotics, and you look at the period, let's say 1950 until now, initially you see a laborious start of the technical methodology, based on a requirement for the soundness of that, drawn up by Alan Turing.

"The Turing test is an experiment, described by Alan Turing in 1936, and further elaborated in his article Computing Machinery and Intelligence (1950) to shed light on the question of whether a machine can display human intelligence.

"The article opens as follows: 'I propose to consider the question: can machines think? This should begin with definitions of the concepts of machine and thinking'. That's difficult, Turing writes. 'Instead of trying to give such a definition, I'll replace the question with another one, which is closely related to it and expressed in relatively unambiguous terms.' Then he proposes the Imitation Game, which has since been called the Turing test:

"In the Imitation Game, an interrogator chats with a man and a woman. The man must pretend to be a woman and the woman must try to prove that the man is an impostor. No computer is involved yet. The first task of the interrogator is to find out who the woman is and who the impostor is. Then the computer is put into the test. It has to take over the role of the man. A computer passes the Turing test when it doesn't make it easier for the interrogator to expose the impostor. It is important during the test that the circumstances are such that it is about intelligence and not about other characteristics such as external appearance; that is why Turing proposes to place the interviewees elsewhere and to allow the exchange of typed text as the only form of communication, via 'teletype' machines - the equivalent of present day chatting.[2]

"At the end of the 1980s, the computer begins to become a familiar phenomenon and you see it in more and more people's homes. It is the time when we were children. When you think of the huge devices that were in companies then! There were special rooms that were used to locate such very large devices. And now you look at your E-watch on your wrist. Bearing in mind that there are 30 years in between, it's logical to wonder what that development will look like in another 30 years, isn't it? Will it continue to grow so steadily, with people keeping control and keeping pace with development? Or are we cultivating a machine that incorporates a principle that is becoming increasingly similar to the algorithm that underlies every human brain?"

"May I interrupt you?" she said. "Here's my first point: I can't go along with all that! You simply assume that there is an algorithm underlying the functioning of the human brain. Who says so?"

"That's what science says. That is, a certain group of scientists says that. There's another group that's trying to prove that the human capacity to think can't be captured in an algorithm."

"I just wanted," she said, "to have an interlocutor who could explain to you at this point the difference between the human capacity to think and the mathematical wonder that is a computer. I sense that there's a world of difference. You don't feel that, but I'm sure you'd be sensitive to sound arguments. Anyway, there's already a point of separation here. Go on ... "

"Even if you assume that no algorithm can be found for human thinking, it is highly probable that an algorithm can be found for the technique of the brain itself, as it functions, independently of human consciousness. Of course, when a person solves problems, he has no insight into what the brain does exactly. Technology can teach us that and science could unlock that part of the technical aspect of the thinking brain. We have come a long way in this direction. Reverse engineering is what it is called. Getting to know thinking."

"No," she said, "a getting to know the physiology, the neurophysiology of the brain during a thought process."

---

[2] From Wikipedia.

"Right. You can perhaps imagine that with this technique we will eventually be able to faithfully imitate in a machine what the human brain physiologically performs during a thought process. With that, one is already a major step along the way."

"Good," she said. "But is there that exponential acceleration in there, too?"

"There doesn't seem to be … " he said, "but that's the characteristic of exponential growth, that it seems to be linear at first, but then it suddenly accelerates in such a way that the graph is almost straight up. That's what we saw in determining the sequence in the DNA molecule. It was thought that it would take a very long time to find out how the human genome is composed. Meanwhile we have the next generation sequencing which brought this process to an almost infinite acceleration; so let me point out that it is now possible for every do-it-yourselfer to determine their own DNA structure in a very short time at home! Something like this could also arise with the development of the computer's thinking ability - and I really do expect that to happen. Once we achieve that acceleration, the expansion of development can no longer be stopped."

"Okay. But what have we actually acquired then?"

"That which cannot be grasped by human thought, will then be grasped. The mathematical processes that a human being cannot perform, can then be accomplished. That opens up a great perspective."

"And you, with your ability to understand, would you want to connect to such a miracle of mathematics – albeit mechanical? Do you think you'll be able to keep your own miraculous power of comprehension alive amid such a violent intervention?"

"These are questions that I can also only ask and cannot answer at this time."

"But you have to look for answers! If what you foresee is really true, then that other side has to be faced! And I don't think you are doing anything about that … "

"Another question," said Els. "Why did your parents actually call you Raymond? Not after that Ray Kurzweil? He was probably already burbling at the time we were born … "

He laughed and said:

"No, they are not at all interested in these things, you know that. I think it's Ray Charles, who I'm actually named after, because that was - and still is - a favourite singer of my parents."

"Georgia on my mind … " she said, "I was supposed to be called Georgia, you know."

"Els is good too!" he said, smiling.

That night she lay awake again. Why was her partner's world of thought so important to her? She'd always known he thought such things, hadn't she? That those ideas went very far? Once she had heard him say that there would come a time when you could upload your brain into a computer, making you immortal. At that time she had thought - or rather, she had comforted herself with the thought - that it was meant to be light-hearted. But she now had to acknowledge that such thought content really lived inside him and that he took those thoughts seriously. Although she had said that she would never leave him, she had a very hard time with it. Why did she care so much about what he thought? Apparently, she thought that what a human being thinks is part of who he really is … And this part she simply didn't want in the man with whom she shared her bed, the dining table and her conversation …

She got up and went to sit in a chair in the living room, with Kurzweil's book in her hands. She read a piece, and got really tired of it. She dozed off a bit in a half sleep and saw the windings of Raymond's brain as a gigantic labyrinth; and in the centre of that labyrinth lived a horribly cruel monster, who had a plan to turn the whole world into a machine. That monster wasn't Raymond himself; and she managed to convince him that this monster had to be removed from the centre of his labyrinth and only he himself could do that. So, he set off and she gave him her love as a guide, so that when he had completed his task he could still find his way out through that labyrinth of brainwashing. She was afraid: he was susceptible to that monster, it might well happen that it would convince him and that he would become one with it. It was a very risky endeavour, this trip to the centre of the labyrinth of Raymond's brain. She couldn't see what he was doing. She felt only, through her love, that he was getting further and further away from her, and when she tugged at the thread of her love, she felt that he was still holding on to it. Oh, let that moment never come when the thread would have come loose or he would have let it go! Then he would be hopelessly lost and the horrible monster would definitively become one with him.

She woke up from her sleep in the chair. She was ice cold. She wanted to cry, but she couldn't find the tears. She wanted to scream, but she didn't want to wake Ray. Despairing, she wondered if there wasn't some paternal figure you could talk to if you sank as deeply into despair as she had now. She crawled into bed with a hot water bottle, slowly warmed up and fell asleep, exhausted.

Two days later they were ambushed by an unexpected event. Raymond came back late from the office. He worked in a large software company and constantly had to live up to his hefty salary as a director. When he entered the room, she saw that something was going on. He was waving a letter, his face betrayed some trouble, although it didn't seem entirely negative.

"What is it?" she said, alarmed.

"I was approached in three different ways today by the Promotor of the Faculty of Artificial Intelligence. First by e-mail, to say that a letter was on its way to me; then I was called whether I had already received the letter. I went to check my postbox at the company and there indeed was that letter - which I thought was weird, because I would have expected such a letter to be sent to someone's home address."

"And what does the letter say?"

"Hang on! They want to nominate me for a chair in 'humanities and artificial intelligence'."

"What?!?" she exclaimed. "Where?"

"Here in Amsterdam."

"But that's fantastic!"

"In a way, it is fantastic. You could say this shows that my complaint that I haven't achieved recognition is being listened to. But first of all, we're going to lose out dramatically in financial terms, because a job, even if it's at the highest level in university education is something quite different from a job in the business world ... "

"I don't care," she objected.

"But secondly, I don't know if I want to be in this field. Look, if I had been asked about the connection between nanotechnology and artificial intelligence, or microbiology and artificial intelligence, I would have cheered. But with this, I would actually land in an alpha faculty and have to research and learn the human sciences as they should be thought of in conjunction with artificial intelligence."

"But isn't that exactly what we were talking about yesterday?" she said.

"Yes, but it's also exactly what I'm least familiar with, isn't it? And, to tell you the truth, what I find the least challenging."

She kept silent and let this change, which could possibly affect their future, come to pass. Suddenly she saw another angle and she said:

"What I see as a drawback is that you'll get completely absorbed in this one topic. You'll be giving lectures, attending congresses, travelling a lot, presenting at conferences – all focused on this topic, and you will still have the opportunity to bring your vision out into the open, in a sense. In any case, you will be working on it even harder than you are now, and I don't see that as something desirable. Why are they asking you?"

"I can understand that," he said. "It is, of course, quite unusual for someone to have studied philosophy as well as having mastered the technical subjects related to artificial intelligence and its development. They know my qualities, my achievements and it must be that it's not been easy to find anyone else."

"You're so young, Raymond!"

"That's not so special these days. The question is: do I want this, can I do this - and do you want it?"

"You've heard," she said. "My initial reaction is immediately: yes, do it right away! My second reaction is my doubts. With you, I believe, it's the other way around. At first you have the impulse: no, I don't want this! And then, of course, in the second instance, the arguments around honour and position, and also of the possibilities, come to the fore … "

"You know," he said, "these days, every step is vital. If I take this step, I will never be able to return to the path of exact science. I will always be associated with the humanities in the alpha faculty. So, if I do this, it will become my lifetime's path."

"You'll have to think about this very carefully and consider all aspects," she said. "And I will do the same … "

"What also is a difficulty," he said, "is that all the teaching, the communication, everything is done in English. I don't really feel like that at all. Philosophy, theology, pedagogy, literature, all these subjects are now brought together in a faculty under the name of 'humanities', which is a superficial 'sweeping up activity', as if they were all of the same substance that you can quietly sweep up together and then give it a common meaning - and that it all has to be enunciated in English! I won't be talking about 'kunstmatige intelligentie' anymore; KI is over, it will always be AI, artificial intelligence. Must I start with that?"

"You speak mostly English in your current work, don't you?"

"That's business, I don't have a problem with that. But to teach in English … "

"You can do that, can't you?"

"I can, but the question is: do I want to?! I think it's a very difficult matter … "

There was still a lot to talk about, but one could keep quiet about it: and that's what they did. They would eat, wash their dishes, check the e-mail, watch some TV and go to bed, without having any idea what answer to give to this question.

When she woke up in the morning, the first question she asked was:

"What are you going to do about that letter?"

"Take it, huh? What else am I going to do? It would be a little strange if I turned this down."

She couldn't imagine what her life with him was going to be like when he became a professor with all those tasks and functions, in a subject which she really wanted to stay away from. She struggled through the day. She had to make a great deal of effort to focus on her patients and their problems. She was exhausted when the day was over.

When Raymond came home, the first thing she asked:

"What are you going to do about that letter?"

"What I told you this morning. I can't say I'm really happy about it, but I have to do it, I can feel it. And maybe I'll come up with a richer range of ideas when I have to explain myself from the professional angle."

"Do you have any idea when this is going to start?

"Not until the new academic year. It's now coming up to Easter; I think the whole application and appointment process should take place this Spring, and I should be in post at the beginning of the new academic year."

"Then I have a question, Raymond."

He looked at her enquiringly and felt a certain desperation in her voice.

"Can't we take a long vacation after you say yes? Go for walks in the mountains and let go of all thoughts of the brain and technique, just looking at the clouds, smelling the flowers in the grass, early in the morning when the dew is still on the leaves, absorbing it all without thinking of synapses and neurons and bits and gigahertz and gigabytes - and goodness knows what else! One wonders how it's possible for the brain to merge that multitude of sensory impressions into an image for you, but try to enjoy that image…. Breathe in the mountain air; maybe, in the distance, the snow is on the peaks; climbing up together until you see ibexes … Will you do that for me?"

He laughed and said:

"Why wouldn't I want to do that? That sounds really wonderful!"

"Yes," she said, "not even thinking about the future, or reflecting on what you've done in the past, but really in the moment, enjoying all the sensory impressions; and being together, so that we can always look back on those memories later on, when things get difficult … "

In her mind's eye she saw his brain: at its centre a monster that wanted to turn all human skills into a machine. The appointment he was now being offered would be a journey to that centre and she would have to make sure that the thread of her love was held firmly in his hands….

The appointment procedure was initiated. Both Els and Raymond looked to the future somewhat gloomily. Els saw how she was going to lose him. Not only could he be completely absorbed in his ideas, but also, the academic world was nowadays run like a company with a management team and the professors were part of that. He would have to undertake a lot of communications work, many meetings in addition, perhaps, also a full lecture programme.

Raymond himself continued to find the fact that he was being appointed to a 'soft' faculty difficult. He had studied philosophy alongside his other studies in order to have an idea, a well-founded insight, into the patterns of thought in the development of mankind. Now it was precisely this study that was to become his main task. But he did not want to reject this calling.

He circulated from one conversation to another, he got to know a large number of people in a short time, including some very significant people. He did enjoy that. He had quit his job at the company and wanted to familiarise himself with the subject over the coming months.

But first, they would go on holiday …

"We really need to get you a new wardrobe!" Els said. "You really can't be a professor in these clothes!"

"Why?" he asked in amazement. "What's wrong with my clothes? I don't see much difference between my outfit and the others."

"There might be more nerds … " she said, smiling.

He looked at her questioningly. What did she mean?

"You guys pick impossible clothes, purple trousers with a yellow checked shirt or something."

He looked at his trousers and his shirt and started laughing.

"What do you mean? What should they be?"

"You'll have to be an example to your pupils in your appearance, too. You can't appear like half a clown at the cathedral. And even among your colleagues you have to show a certain dignity."

"Well I don't seem to have much of a dress sense … " he said. "So you'll have to be my style advisor and I'll wear whatever you buy."

Els was a fashion-conscious type. She paid close attention to her figure, went to the hairdresser every month to get her hair blonde, wore it half-long or in a ponytail. She dressed very carefully and wore half classic trendy clothes. Of course, he enjoyed the fact that she looked good, but he had never thought about how he looked himself. Naturally, he sometimes looked in the mirror, but he didn't really like what he saw there, so he returned to his world of thought, to his intelligence.

"I don't have to buy a whole set of suits, do I?"

"For certain occasions, I think that's important. But in everyday life at university it's best to appear in a pair of trousers and a shirt, or trousers and a sweater. But it has to be appropriate … "

"If it's been so terrible," he said, "why are you only telling me this now?"

"I've told you before, but you were not listening!"

She ate into his bank account by dragging him around the city shops for three days, looking for suitable clothes. His shoes had to be changed too, and actually she thought he should have his hair cut differently as well.

He accepted all this, knowing that there was nothing wrong with her taste; and he also noticed that there was a different reaction to him when he started wearing these new clothes.

They booked a flight to Switzerland and rented a house from a colleague of Els'. There they would stay for a month and when they came back he would dive straight into his new work.

It was a large Swiss chalet, much too big for two people, with a large sloping garden around it and a beautiful view over the valley. A bit further down the road was a hotel with a restaurant where they could have a nice meal and even breakfast when they wanted to have it easy.

The first evening was filled with making themselves at home in the house, eating in the restaurant and going to bed early after their tiring journey and the busy days before they left.

But the next day …

It was still quite cold so high up in the mountains. You could sit in the sun against the outside wall but it was too cold, for example, to sit in the garden. After breakfast they went shopping. But then …

They had agreed to only look twice a day at their mobile phones and nothing else. They also agreed not to watch TV, not to read professional literature, only to walk, take pictures and read literature, and of course to be together.

As they were sitting outside on the terrace with a cup of coffee he said:

"Els, I have to admit: I'm a workaholic!"

"Me too," she said.

"How empty this all is! What on earth are you supposed to do with your life when you're not allowed to work or be with your circle of friends?"

"It doesn't seem possible just to be ourselves in nature anymore," she said. "I feel that very clearly here. We want letters, numbers, images of light, continuous feeding for that stimulation - and when you see such images of light in real life, you find them boring! They always remain the same, except when you turn your head or when you go for a walk; then of course it does change, but not at the speed and rate you are used to. This is what they call 'relaxing' in the hotel world, I believe. We're living under constant pressure and don't know what it's like to not be in a hurry for once and just be - where we are."

"The question is," he said, "whether that's necessary. I find it an extraordinarily unpleasant feeling."

"Your first sentence was, 'I think I'm a workaholic.' You're actually agreeing that it's something negative, this constant rushing from one impression to another."

"That's just the way it is … " he admitted.

He sighed and said:

"Then let's go for a walk. You're well organised, you've been mapping out all kinds of routes, so we can start right away."

"There's one route," she said, "that passes right here by the house, so we can do that first. It's not that long either, because we'll have to build up our physical fitness. This walk runs quite horizontally and goes past mountain meadows and woods."

"I think walking is boring," he said, "but okay … "

They put on their mountain boots, took a backpack with some food and drinks and a walking stick for potentially difficult stretches, and set off.

69

Els had printed out the route, because she didn't want to look at her mobile all the time. They put the mobile phones in the backpack …

At first the road went through a wooded area, at the edge of which a view of the mountain range on the other side of the valley opened up. They stopped, he took a deep breath and said:

"How majestic! I'm quite impressed by that … You tend to want to breathe in and out very deeply, as if your lungs wished to be as big as the volume of the valley below … "

Els laughed and said:

"You could even become a poet! 'The poetic professor', on the pattern of, let's say, Schiller."

"I know of him only as the author of certain philosophical human insights?"

"He was a poet, too." Els said.

They walked further along the still wide path, right through a mountain meadow dotted with flowers, both known and unknown to them. Els stopped once in a while and picked a few flowers.

"Is that allowed?" he said. "Maybe you're robbing nature of rare species!"

"Yes, it's okay."

"I'd like to know what they're all called … What are all these things?"

"What do you care?" she said. "Look, you know what these 'things' are, don't you? Even if you don't know the names. You see the colours, you see whether they're tall or short, whether they are strong or not, how they are coloured - the leaves, but especially the flowers - you can look at that, can't you?"

"What do I care about the name?" he echoed, somewhat moodily. "I always want to know what it is!"

"Do you know something if you simply know the name?" she asked grumpily.

He grabbed her hand and they continued happily. Occasionally they stopped because Els saw some new flowers she wanted to add to her bouquet.

"If you need to hold on to a rock, you'll be sorry you have those flowers in your hands!"

"No, this road is completely flat, so that's not going to happen to us!"

70

Once in a while they met other people. Some of them walked by look-ing silently ahead of them. Els always said, 'Gruss Gott!' Sometimes they would say something in return, but there were also passers-by who gave a cheerful greeting of their own accord.

Raymond asked:

"Why do you say 'Grüss Gott'? They don't say it here at all. They say 'Guten Tag' or something, but I haven't heard anyone say 'Grüss Gott' yet. Which God do you mean?"

"Don't be silly. You know that in southern Germany and Austria it's a traditional greeting to say 'Grüss Gott', and it's an appropriate greeting when you're walking in nature…..that you're experiencing something divine in it, whether you can still believe in it or not. You said yourself a moment ago that you are sensing the majesty of nature. Let us then genuinely feel that and share it with our fellow walkers when we meet and say: 'Grüss Gott' - even if they don't say it here, they really do un-derstand."

"Well, you always come up with an answer!"

"I don't think you'd be satisfied with someone who didn't have any-thing to say!"

After two hours of walking, they were exhausted. They felt their knees, ankles, back and shoulders. Everything began to show signs of fatigue, but they had to walk for at least another hour.

"How's your boredom now?" she asked. "Do you still feel that it is boring?"

"In a way," he said, "it's getting worse, because my body doesn't want to do any more. But on the other hand, you also notice that you are now redirecting your need for fulfilment to keeping your body upright. You have to use your energy to get home, so that in itself is interesting … " he said.

"Oh, no!"

"I mean in terms of self-knowledge, that you feel as a human being that you are something more than just a brain. You could forget that at home, at work … "

"I can never forget that," she said. "Because it's rare for a patient to have a brain-related problem. Most of the diseases lie completely else-where … "

They went for a walk every day, every day a bit further, a bit higher. Their physical condition improved tremendously and life in the 'world of data' became a thing of the past. Raymond also stopped saying that he found it boring, he began to feel the benefits of nature in his physical condition. His thoughts did not stand still, but they were changing. More and more it was sensory impressions that filled his thoughts.

In the evening, when he sat on the couch with a book in his hand, by the fire, accompanied by a glass of wine, he felt intensely happy.

They didn't talk about singularity - neither about the digital information in the cosmos, nor about his future job. As far as he was concerned, all that could be postponed indefinitely. This was real life, and he examined his own thoughts with amazement. You would want to become a farmer or a gardener or a retiree ... and spend the rest of your life in nature. How could he ever have thought that it's always the same there? It wasn't the same for a second! Every step he took brought a change in the picture, the perception of the environment he was in. He observed with awe how wonderful that was.

Not that he doubted his vision, but he found this a great preparation for his work in the Faculty of Humanities. He had been introduced to a new world and he was certainly going to succeed in relating what he was now absorbing as a sensory reality with his brain, to his original vision. He had no notion at all of what that was going to look like, but he felt that there was still a great deal to explore there. These were not concrete thoughts, he did not want to occupy himself with them now, but it did make him feel more at home in his new role.

After a week the situation changed again. Storms and deluges of rain blew through - as bad as it can get only in the mountains. That too was impressive, but it ensured they couldn't go hiking and had to spend whole days in the house. It was not easy to keep their hands off the equipment and also not to sit in front of the TV.

They got up later in the day, made an extensive breakfast, spent some time sorting out the household, and hoped for better weather.

Els said:

"My colleague told me there's a cultural centre somewhere here, where there's a lot of music, recitals, recitation. It seems to be mainly Dutch people who are active there. She also said: if the weather is bad, it's nice to go there for an evening, if there's something you're interested in. The programme can be found on the Internet."

"All right … Is it far from here?"

"I don't know, let's have a look … "

Being disciplined people, they didn't grab their device straight away, but waited for the pre-agreed time to use their daily ration of internet access …

She found the name and then the address.

"No, it's not far away at all. It's a few hundred metres below us. I think we passed it. There are two concerts this week and two lectures. One is about the science of thinking. I think that's a possibility, maybe you'd get some ideas from it."

"It must be very superficial!" he grumbled. "You can't expect to find a top speaker in a corner like this. But as a break from our experiences of nature here, I think it would be interesting, yeah."

"There are also Bach's violin partitas one evening, that might be worthwhile?'"

"First, let's try this lecture and then we'll see … " he said. "I don't feel the need to get involved with a Dutch community here."

"It doesn't look like that," she said. "The impression is much more Swiss. Anyway, you're right, let's take a look."

They drove down through storm and heavy rainfall a few hundred meters with their small rental car and found the entrance to the centre which was situated in a large park with beautifully landscaped gardens, and also with large stretches of natural mountain scenery. At the end of the road was a large nineteenth century, or perhaps early twentieth century, building with some Jugendstil features, with a car park in front of it packed with cars.

"Strange, you'd say you're in a remote area here. A bit off the road like that, and suddenly a lot of people come together. It makes me wonder," Raymond grumbled. He didn't really feel like joining a group of people who were perhaps busy with various unknown preoccupations. But on the other hand, he also felt the need to do something else now that they couldn't go for walks.

"Look!" said Els, "there's also a very big restaurant! We could eat there some time, it looks very inviting."

The atmosphere radiated outwards through the busyness. There were a lot of people about and you could hear the cheerfulness from outside.

They went into the lobby, saw a reception desk and asked for the location where the lecture would be. The receptionist was very friendly, not Dutch but 'real Swiss'. She walked out in front of them to show the room where the lecture would be held. It was a kind of theatre with a stage, but the lectern was in front of the stage. The hall was half full; there were maybe fifty people there.

"How is it possible" exclaimed Raymond, "that there is so much interest?"

"Yes, my colleague also said that there is a really interesting bunch of people who are working here, and that a lot of people from abroad come to stay for a while. Apparently, there is also a first aid post for hikers in summer and skiers in winter, because the hospital is quite far away and if anything happens they take care of the first aid … "

"Is there also a clinic?"

" Yes, a small one, indeed, but with a real first aid post - a doctor's post you could say."

They found a place in the middle of the room, where they had a good view of the lectern, and took their seats.

Gradually the room filled up completely. It was clear that there were people who felt quite at home here, but that there were also passers-by like themselves.

Raymond thought: A lecture on the science of thinking: who would be interested in that? He thought: it must be a lecture about reverse engineering, what else should it be? A lecture on the neurophysiological knowledge of the brain. For him it was the foundation, but he was still curious as to how it would be presented here, in a mountainous area in Switzerland, far away from any university. He actually found it a bit exciting, and he said to Els:

"It's crazy, Els, it's making me a bit nervous!"

"Me too! See how quickly you become a stranger to the world. We've only been out of the digital city world for a week … "

"Could it be that?"

" Seems to me like it … "

"Well, we'll see. I'm slightly uncomfortable … "

Their gaze was drawn by a man coming in. A fine specimen of mankind … Clearly of Indian descent, timeless … Probably about eighty years old anyway. A beautiful bunch of thick grey hair. Dressed in a priestly anthracite suit. He entered the room together with a much younger woman, a beautiful woman, probably in her late forties, who impressed by her appearance of agility.

"Those are two rare personalities!" Raymond said to Els.

"Yes indeed … " she said. "I am astonished by this, too. Where do you see people like that – such individual characters?"

They took their seats in the front row and a few other remarkable people came in and sat down in the front row.

Raymond whispered to Els:

"That's definitely the management team here!"

"I don't think that's what they call it here … " she said. "Anyway, it must be something like that."

It went quiet. The institute's clock struck eight. The silence grew deeper and deeper. When Raymond thought: this silence can't get any deeper … … an older man came in, once fair-haired, now slightly greying. A tall figure, a beautiful face, a more impressive appearance than all the striking figures in the first row put together …

A shiver ran down his spine and he felt that nervousness again. Who were these people who could impress you so much?

The old man - Raymond corrected himself and thought: he's a lot older than I am, but whether I'll still appear as young as I am now when I'm as old as he is….. he must be in his sixties, but he has the appearance of a lively young man – the man had no notes with him and walked towards the lectern. He looked quietly around the room and began to speak, without using notes.

From the very first words he uttered with his sonorous voice, calm and deliberate, Raymond was certain: this man knows I'm here and he is speaking directly to me.

Initially the speaker presented statements that seemed to be entirely in line with Raymond's vision. He spoke about the need for a science of thought technique. Raymond had difficulty understanding the German, although he knew the language well. Perhaps it was not the language, but the older man's way of speaking. His voice was pleasant, he had a clear eloquent voice, he was evidently accustomed to speaking in public and did so in a rather relaxed and comprehensible way. And yet Raymond kept losing the thread. At one point he got the feeling that there was an acceleration, as one can witness when an aeroplane accelerates during take-off, and then releases itself from the earth with tremendous force. Something similar happened in this lecture and Raymond got the annoying feeling that he could just about follow the train of thought, when it was still 'connected to the earth'; but once it had become airborne, he completely lost its thread. He heard the words, heard the sentences, heard the connections, but he did not grasp their meaning. For a man as highly intelligent as he was, this was a kind of torture. He had the feeling: this speaker grabbed me by my intelligent guts and boxed me around my ears, right, left, and right, until I was dizzy. He didn't make a bad impression - on the contrary: it was obvious that he was an amiable man, erudite too; but he could not follow it, he did not understand it. What he said had some resemblance with philosophy, perhaps with the 'prima philosophia', but it wasn't that, either. He talked about thinking, in so far as that doesn't happen through the brain. He heard that. But what he then explained about it, completely eluded him. This powerlessness gradually made Raymond angry, until he was furious. How could somebody speak for an hour, coherently, deliberately, clearly audibly, but absolutely without perceivable content? When the man stopped speaking after an hour, he briefly caught his eye. Oh yes, this man had deliberately spoken like that in order to teach him a lesson. But he hadn't even understood the lesson, so he couldn't learn anything from it!

The people around them got up and gradually left the room. Some of them stayed at the front to converse with the speaker, with the Indian man and with the younger woman and the others who clearly belonged to that group. He felt a razor-sharp animosity rising towards this 'bunch of pampered vagrants'!
Els wanted to get up too, but he stopped her.
"Wait a minute," he said, "I don't want to have to go through there … "
She sat down again and they waited until everyone had left the room.

They didn't know that once, years ago, the speaker had himself been sitting like that in this room too, after a lecture by the oriental man.

That he also had felt - he had understood the message - that he had been completely confused and had remained seated until a girl from outside had come in to ask him if he was all right. It was a kind of repetition of that event, albeit in a very different atmosphere. The same girl - now a mature woman - was the younger woman who had entered the room together with the oriental man; she entered the room and came across to him as if she had to play the scene over again.

She looked at him and asked;

"Are you all right?"

He looked into her blue eyes and became despondent, like a balloon from which the air was being released. He said, dully:

" Yes, yes … I have to process this, but it's not that important."

The woman looked at him inquisitively and didn't believe any of that 'unimportance'. She said in Dutch;

"I hear you're Dutch. So are we. I am Eva Leven and I work here as a doctor in the clinic."

She shook hands with him; she shook hands with Els as well.

"If you would like to speak to my husband - "

"Your husband?" Raymond said in a lethargic tone.

"Yes, that's the man who just gave the lecture. If you need to speak to him, you can always call for an appointment. Here's his card."

He took it and hoped she'd leave now, whatever else she did.

"Come on," he said to Els, "let's go!"

In the car, Els at the wheel, said:

"So! You were angry!"

"Yeah, what am I going to do with a bullshit story like that! A handsome fellow, with a great mind, selling such nonsense!"

"Tell me what that bullshit was?" She suspected he hadn't heard a word of it, she knew him so well!

She parked the car at their chalet and they went inside.

"Well, dear Raymond, spill your beans! I'm not so sure it was a good idea to go there."

"Maybe it was … " he said. "Well, I wouldn't be able to repeat what that guy's been preaching. At first, I thought what he said made sense. But then, as far as I was concerned, he let go of all rationality and ascended into areas where there's no reality. I got incredibly angry that it's possible for someone to attract a hundred people to tell a 'bullshit story!' "

Els took a deep breath and said:

"It's a shame you can't seem to sense quality - with your quantitative thinking!"

He laughed and said:

"That's another real Els remark! What kind of quality? He stood there discoursing about thought processes that are separate from the brain. How did he come up with such nonsense?"

Els saw the image of the labyrinth and how the black monster in the centre scored points. Oh, he's stuck in this world of thought. How was she supposed to answer, so as not to make it worse? She herself had listened to this man with amazement. For her, it had been a great feast of artistic thought. For her there was no doubt that what he spoke was the truth. It was another aspect of being human that he had revealed, which she herself intuitively knew existed. This had also been her argument against Raymond's vision of the future; the source of her nightly fears lay in the opposite direction. And she knew that the important thing now was how she would react. This was a turning point in his life: either he would definitely turn away from this other aspect of being human with all the vehemence he could exhibit, in which case life with him would become unbearable; or he would be brought into a state of doubt. The question was what to say now. She let herself be guided by her intuition and said:

"Okay, I totally understand. Of course, this story does not fit in at all with the vision of the future of Man as you have built it up over the years; and this makes you furious, I understand that very well. But maybe now the 'other' Raymond wants to appear again, who is in there too, who may be stunned by this 'bullshit story' that he can't even follow, but who knows very well that the man who said all that, is not crazy! That he is also a very special person, you know damn well. Let that side of you speak out for once!"

He stood up and kneeled before her, took her hands in his and said:

"My dearest Els, will you marry me?"

She was perplexed. He didn't want to marry, he didn't want children, he just wanted science - and she was allowed to be there for his enjoyment in his free time...But then indeed he was also this other Raymond ...

With big eyes and open-mouthed she looked at him and exclaimed:

78

"What the hell!"

"I can't sink any lower, Els, I'm at the nadir now, on my knees. Will you marry me?!"

She pulled him up and hugged him, and said:

"There's nothing I'd rather do!! But you're avoiding my question!"

They sat next to each other on the sofa, cuddled together, and he said:

"It's really all interconnected, Els. It's that 'other' Raymond who's just asked you to marry him and who really means it, from the bottom of his heart. And that one … yeah, he has to admit that his giftedness, his so-called great intelligence, is no match for an argument like the one we've just heard. I just can't follow it, I don't understand it. What is that man talking about? And it wouldn't be such big deal if it wasn't that man! You're absolutely right, he is a quite remarkable person. Though I don't understand a letter of it, I do feel he's truthful, much more truthful than many a scientist I know. So, what am I supposed to do with all this? I'd prefer to turn back the clock to a day ago and then make the decision not to go to that lecture, so that I can quietly continue on the treadmill of trusted thinking."

"That other Raymond doesn't mean that, either … " she said.

He sighed deeply and said:

"No, but I really don't know what to do with all this."

"The lady said we could request a meeting with him."

"It would be a catastrophe. I'd have to know what the hell he's talking about, first!"

"Then – let's go to another lecture," she said.

"Oh my God, I thought we were supposed to be out here enjoying nature!"

"That's what I thought, too. And now we're almost married, and we've hit upon a path in nature that I believe grows completely *out* of nature. But not one heading towards neurons and synapses and billions of data that can be stored and retrieved, but a path that seems to want to let go of all those numbers and magnitudes."

"Hold me tight, because it scares the hell out of me … " he said.

Again, she saw the black monster in the centre of his labyrinth. But it withdrew and had to admit that it hadn't yet scored any points, maybe even lost some. She felt infinitely sorry for the walker in the labyrinth. So many qualities and so attached to finiteness…

*

The next day it rained again, but now they had no trouble filling the hours. After breakfast they sat together at the table and made plans for their wedding. They picked a date, thought of a programme for the special day, wondered what a suitable location would be and above all: who they wanted to invite. That turned into a big group; they both had a lot of family, and many friends, girlfriends and colleagues. The strange thing was that they had never been able to take that final step of bonding with each other. Now that step had been taken and there was no trace of doubt to be found. It woke them up, it made them happy and joyful.

So, during that rainy weather a good-natured warm bright sun was shining. The only cloud in the sky for Raymond was that man there, a few hundred meters down the road. Els said:

"I know that man from somewhere - I've seen his picture, and I'm wondering where … It must have been in Holland, because I haven't seen any pictures here … "

"You just have to look on the internet and then you'll know who he is. Of course, that's no problem; he must have written books too, in which you can read that vague nonsense again."

"Stop it, Raymond! You're a scientist and a scientist doesn't declare as nonsense what he doesn't know!"

"Ah, there's Els again!" he smiled. "If anyone else said something like that to me, I'd get furious. But from you, I only like it … "

"Especially since you don't have to take it seriously!"

"No, no," he said, "I do take it very seriously. I value your judgment very much, you know that … "

They had agreed to drive there one more evening at the end of the week to attend a second lecture by this man.

"I just wish I could prepare for it," Raymond said, "so that I could at least sit there and understand the meaning of what he's saying. I should be able to do that, shouldn't I? I am so practised in abstract thinking, you would say, that when that thinking takes flight high above the earth like an aeroplane, I should be able to follow it. You can do that. Why can't I?"

She knew very well why he couldn't. He had had abstract thoughts from the cradle, so to speak, but in numbers and letters and in syllables, and not in the sort of thoughts which you needed to think artistically. She had an idea, and said:

"If you think of a prelude and fugue by Bach - a real fugue, not a fake copy - you have content there that you don't calculate before you play it, but you read the content in the notes and you're able to perform what you've read with your hands. It's not a text, it's not a calculation - and yet one is saying something … "

"Music is calculable, you know! They already knew that in antiquity, but nowadays that arithmetic in music is of course much more precise and refined."

"I'm sure … " Els said.

He looked at her attentively and said:

"But I can't listen to a lecture consisting of text as though I'm listening to Bach, can I? I'll not be hearing music, I'll be hearing the spoken word - and that's what I want to understand."

"That's clear," she said. "I mean more the nature of listening than the content. You've been listening since you were in the cradle to cultivated quantitative thinking. 'Everything can be calculated. That's why the human brain, in so far as it can be calculated, can be uploaded into the computer in due course.' With that sort of thinking, you can't possibly follow that man."

"So his thinking is incalculable!"

Els laughed and said:

"Yes, literally! What he says has nothing to do with the observation of nature, nothing to do with knowing technology, and I am convinced that if you let go of your resistance – yes, your antipathy - you would understand him. Though you would probably be very shaken by what he says and then maybe get angry about it again."

"Tricky fellow, that Raymond," he said with self-mockery.

"I don't know if you should call that tricky. You just got so big and now you're stuck with it. You've stuffed yourself with numbers and formulas and thoughts that go with it. Isn't it true that you can only do that because of a certain antipathy? That you push it off, as it were, and then you see it all from the outside and can copy it, put it into the system, analyse it and so on. This man really speaks out of sympathy; I think that's where the problem lies."

"Am I a man with that much antipathy?"

Els said:

"No, you're very kind, I love you the way you are, you know that. Otherwise I wouldn't be marrying you … But, of course, it's because I love you so much that I can see your one-sidedness."

"And that man has the other one-sidedness?"

"I wouldn't put it that way," she said. "In my experience of musical and psychological harmony, there is no such thing as one-sidedness. Sympathy can be all-sided, can't it? In that respect I agree with Teilhard de Chardin."

"If I listen to you," he said, "I can understand what you're saying. Why am I so completely lost when I have to listen to that man? I'm confronted with a piece of *inadequacy* in me. Of course, that scares the hell out of me. And my intelligence is one-sided … !"

"Not originally, it seems to me. You're not a nerd like that. But your life's journey has been such that you've also been encouraged to be one-sided. Your parents cultivated and stimulated that and the teachers who were present on your path did not feel that they had to deflect something, had to supplement it. You fit in with modern times and you are an excellent example of these modern times. You see: at 34 years of age, you are already becoming a professor, you have already held a director's post in a large software company, you play on the grand piano as if you were on the concert stage! Who would say that Raymond is unilaterally gifted!"

"But then you can understand that being confronted by these incomprehensible ways of thinking has been a draining experience for me. Now we have agreed that I will expose myself to this again on Friday and I would so like to know: How do I prepare myself now, so that it doesn't happen to me a second time?"

"I told you, but maybe you didn't listen….. Sympathy instead of antipathy; that is, to stay attentive, surrender to what someone is actually saying - without wanting to put your own vision up against it. And

82

listening as if you were listening to Bach. Then you don't have to think: 'those five bars: I would have written them differently, myself!' "

He burst out laughing.

"That synthetic Bach piece, you may be able to calculate it all very well, but the real Bach… Do not think that it can be caught in a calculation! And so it is with the thinking of that man down there. He thinks and expresses his thoughts the way they are inimitable and incalculable in his life."

"Who are you?" he asked in amazement. "How do you know all this?"

Els sighed, she felt deeply moved.

"I don't know!" she said. "It's my love for you and for your giftedness that makes me say this, I think. You know, I'm shocked by your vision of the future. I can't comprehend how you genuinely believe in that at all - "

"I really do!"

"Yeah, that one Raymond, he believes in that, of course. But the other one, he has yet to speak. And I find it really surprising that we've travelled here to be in nature, that we want to occupy ourselves with a lecture - and that this lecture has exactly the content that could wake up that other Raymond!"

It cleared up a bit and at least it was dry when they drove down the road for the second time, to go through the gate to the gardens and park the car in the car park. It smelled nice and fresh, everywhere the birds whistled joyfully over the clearing, and veils of fog were lifting … .

"If this is an image for what we're about to experience, then I'm hopeful." Els said.

"I'm imagining it as though it were a mountain! A mountain that is much higher than all the mountains around here, one that can be thought of as part of the highest mountain ranges. Even higher is the mountain that I am imagining."

"I understand … " she said and took his hand.

They went inside, now they knew their way around and entered the room. They sat down in about the same places again.

Again, the room was about half filled with people waiting. Again, the now familiar radiant and powerful group of people came and sat down in the front row. Again, the clock on the building struck eight and again the older man came in punctually.

Once again, he looked in the direction of Raymond and Els and again Raymond felt: he knows I am here and what he is going to say, he is saying to me especially … .

"Dear friends, ladies and gentlemen! We have now been working here for about twenty years presenting lectures and courses and, naturally, one can't give the same lecture twice a week for twenty years! We have touched on many subjects, and we have done this year in and year out building on the power of the spiritualisation of thought.

"Many of you have been here from the very beginning, but probably as many of you will be hearing a lecture tonight, or on one of these evenings, for the first time. On the one hand I try not to bore the advanced - on the other hand I try to interest the newcomers … "

So far it was not difficult to follow. The plane was still firmly stationary on the ground. The man continued:

"When I talk about a science of thought, I'm not talking about the scientific neurophysiology of the brain, which increasingly identifies which parts of the brain do exactly what. This knowledge is becoming more and more sophisticated, diversifying and becoming a highly specialised field of brain analysis.

"The research I am talking about is of an entirely different kind. It is not about brain research, but - in the first instance – about becoming aware that as a human being you are thinking and that you are developing a skill to refine this - within that general observation of 'I am a thinking being' - by getting to know within yourself the functioning of intelligence. It's not about what the brain does; it's about being able to know what you're doing while you're thinking."

He could still follow this and so far he didn't think it was nonsense. It was even a little intriguing, as to where this argument would lead…

The man continued:

"When you look at the physiology of the body, you can say that medical science has made great advances in examining the physical-chemical processes in the human body. For example, the function of the liver is well known, both with regard to the build-up of substances and with regard to the detoxification that takes place in the liver and the breaking down of the blood. Of course, you could never say that as a human being you can know for yourself how your own liver functions. There is a science about the liver function and no one would want to say from the ordinary scientific community that as a thinking human being, as a knowing human being, that you can consciously experience those processes in the liver yourself. The extent to which you yourself are involved in these processes is unclear, but you would never say that you yourself know exactly how to break down the blood and have the breakdown products discharged into the intestines via the bile. It is very important to be aware of this. If you look at the physiology of the nervous system, this also applies to a major proportion of the processes that take place on the basis of this nervous system.

"When you *think about thinking* in relation to the brain, you are dealing with a function in which it becomes possible for the researcher to determine very precisely how the rules in thinking are followed. Here you have activity in the brain in the same way that you have functioning in the liver. While there is no possibility of having an awareness of what a liver is doing, it is possible to have an awareness of what thinking is doing. You cannot know - by analogy with the liver - what the brain is doing. But while you can't know your own liver processes either with, or without a liver, you can know the thought processes without a brain."

It became more difficult for Raymond. He wanted to call out: 'Hold still for a moment, so I can think this over again!' But, of course, he couldn't, he would have to do that later, and the question was whether he would still know what it was about. Because somehow his memory didn't want him to do this, either. He shouldn't have too many thoughts of his own, because then the lecturer would be so far ahead that he would have to let go - and that really wasn't supposed to happen this time!

Something was bothering him … The difference between the consciousness of the liver processes and the consciousness of the thinking processes …

"I am not speaking," said the man, "about the thoughts that just randomly come to mind in us, not about the memories that come looming up, not about the thoughts that every human being can have, not about the castles in the sky that you can build. I am talking about intelligent thinking. As soon as a human being thinks intelligently, he himself is fully involved in it. It is impossible to think intelligent thoughts without being present. That's why intelligence so easily creates a sense of pride in the intelligent person. As the owner of a well-functioning liver - you don't feel any personal pride in that. But a good set of brains - curiously, without question! – is something people are indeed proud of! When thinking intelligent thoughts, the thinker is fully involved. He creates them himself, and although the awareness of them must be awakened, the thinker also knows through and through how these thoughts and the connection between the concepts are created, and how that connection relates to truth or untruth. Sooner or later every human being who wants to focus inwardly on this will become aware that there is nothing in existence on earth, which one knows as well as the production of one's own intelligent thoughts and concepts. For that, one doesn't need brain physiology at all. That can shed light on how the brain gives a physical existence to that which man himself produces - not with the body, but really himself - and whose cohesion and relations he fully examines. The fact that not every human being is naturally aware of this – one's own production of intelligent thoughts and the complete insight into their coherence and relations - is because these are processes that are not in the area of the functioning of the brain. The brain registers the thoughts, but the brain cannot register how the thinker is working in it with his knowledge. Therefore, brain physiology will always be able to record only the thought facts and not man's deeper knowledge regarding the functioning of his own intelligence."

Again, it dazzled him. His honest side told him: 'This is dazzling you because you register the truth of these words flawlessly, and this truth is completely overturning your view of the world'. His proud vision of the future, on the other hand, said to him: 'This is old hat, this is the conquered prima philosophia. The ancient Greek Aristotle described all this in his logic - he couldn't have had a clue about brain physiology. There will surely come a time when science will in addition be able to prove what this man says is now impossible. Science will show that everything that human intelligence produces is a product of brain activity'. He was dizzy and he really had to make every effort not to fall into some kind of dream sleep.

In the meantime, the man continued to speak.

"The first person in his time who, as far as was possible, gave a clear description of this knowing of thought was the great philosopher Aristotle. In the many centuries that followed, the thinkers practised the art of thinking on the basis of his writings. Especially in the period of scholasticism it was an honour to make thinking so clear and sharp that not a single unexplained point remained in a thought process. This then passed into science as the basis of the experiment. The inner clarification of thought has, as it were, fallen asleep, to be awakened in our time. But then, of course, in our time, that consciousness of being the thinker and of knowing the thinking technique thoroughly has itself changed. We cannot go back to Aristotle, we cannot go back to scholasticism, we cannot go back to the German idealists, such as Hegel, Fichte and others. It's not about rewriting logic, it's not about thinking logic over internally. That still wouldn't differ that much from getting acquainted with liver physiology or brain physiology. It would still be a science that stands at a distance from you and can be learned by heart. So - you can't say then that you produce the intelligent think- ing yourself and therefore know thoroughly its coherence and internal relationships. It is not about the number of scientific facts at all.

"Because you cross a certain boundary here from body physiology to self-consciously being active in thinking, it becomes proportionally difficult to express what you actually have to say about this."

Yeah, yeah! Thought Raymond, that's a nice excuse. When you leave the realm of facts, it is very easy to say: 'the area we are entering now cannot be described'. He then had to come to the conclusion that this man leads the listener in a very rational way to a point where all reason is abandoned.

But the man said:

"I'll try to describe this new area in a very factual way. The bridge to it lies in the contemplation of one's own self. It is a mysterious fact that every human being calls himself 'I' and then knows exactly what he or she means by that. Now, of course, the easiest thing to say is that it indicates your physical existence. But when you go beyond this brief and easy observation, other perspectives arise. Descartes said, "I think, therefore I am." Apparently, he felt that the self has something to do with thinking, if not everything! When you look strictly at the physical this statement is nonsense, because when you lie in bed at night and sleep it is clear that you don't think, but that the body is still there, only it can't say 'I' anymore. But if the body were the self, then you would exclude self-awareness completely from that 'I'. After all, it wouldn't matter if that self-awareness was there or not, because self-conscious- ness would also be there without it. There lies an interesting point of reflection on the self.

"A second point is the question: how do I know I exist? Here, too, the shortest and easiest answer is: the fact that I have a body makes that clear to me!

"But when you try to find out in the thinking itself whether you exist as 'I', then you come to interesting discoveries, and these are not limited to a description of a fact, but that fact is actually experienced.

"I would like to point out once again that it is quite possible to bypass this explanation entirely by an exclusively body-physiological approach. But this completely excludes what man experiences of his intelligent thought processes.

"If one wants to develop an awareness of precisely that, then it is necessary not to think about the body processes for once and only to retreat into initiating and carrying out a coherent thought process, and experiencing it. The self has a knowing that it exists there. Not only the thoughts exist, but the one who is thinking exists much more intensively. That is the presence in every human being, which makes a highly gifted intelligent person proud of himself or herself, because he or she unconsciously knows that he or she is present as someone who is controlling the production of intelligent thought processes through and through. It's much the same as being impressed when an artist - a musician - performs an extraordinarily complex piece of music fluently and demonstrates that he or she is above and beyond any technical difficulties. Thus, the thinker is above the technical difficulties of thinking, because the thinking itself is in no way different from the thinker."

This time the airplane did not take off, although the thinking was certainly not earthbound. Raymond could have followed every thought from start to finish, but at the end of the lecture he had to come to the conclusion for himself: I may have been able to follow these thoughts, but that I can also produce them myself and thoroughly control their coherence - I cannot see that.

*

He just walked past the people in the front row, past the man who had given the lecture, out of the hall, Els behind him.

He retreated into himself, sat down at the wheel, drove up the hill and Els made no contact with him. Once in bed she took his hand and that's how they fell asleep.

90

When she woke up the next morning she had the memory of a horrible dream in which Raymond deliberately united with the monster in the centre of his labyrinth. He also deliberately let go of the thread. She had lost him …

But when they were having breakfast, everything was very normal and cosy. Not a word was said about the lecture, and her attempts to raise the subject failed. She also noticed that he was constantly lost in his own thoughts and not attentive to what she said or did. Even when he was reading a book she still had the impression that he wasn't reading the book, but that he was engrossed in his own thoughts.

It made her desperate and she would have preferred to have said to him: 'Never mind the marriage, let's just go on in the way we've always been together. If at some point I want to leave you, at least it's not such a mess' -. But she didn't say anything, because she felt sorry for him and she loved that child prodigy who had gone astray. She knew that if she had been his mother, she would have taken measures to keep him on the ground in order to keep his thoughts connected to reality.

Now he had become so accustomed to abstract thinking that he did not need to have anything to do with an observable reality, so it would be very difficult to call him back from it.

She herself reflected with amazement on last night's lecture. For her it had been a kind of logical revelation, as if her deepest knowledge had been expressed by someone else, because she could only become aware of it that way … But what was she to do with her deepest insights next to a man like him? And luring him away from his entanglement seemed impossible. At first, she had retained some hold on him, but now it seemed as if he had slammed the door shut completely. He retreated completely into himself and was only prepared to communicate with her in an everyday atmosphere. If only she could go to that man down there in that institute, to talk to him and ask him to communicate …

But they were together every second, they even went grocery shopping together, so there was no way of getting in touch with that man without his knowledge.

Luckily the weather cleared up and they could go for a walk again, which made them both think about other things. Nature was refreshed by all that rain. They themselves felt like they were in a catastrophe.

Raymond had indeed slammed the door with a bang. He had stored the thoughts he had gathered during the lecture somewhere in a hidden cupboard inside and had closed the door with the intention of never opening it again! He justified this by arguing that it was all just philosophy that was long outdated and that that man, expressing all these thoughts, really had no idea about the scientific development of his time; for him, time had stood still. But for Raymond his approach was something he didn't go along with.

Yet it was difficult for him to shut out the fragments of thought that had leaked out of the cupboard - which was so securely closed. They rose up in his consciousness like demons and asked him, as it were: 'Look at us and compare us to your usual thoughts! And then look how one thing differs from another and what that means?!'

It was the phenomenon of associative memory that bothered him. He didn't want to think any more about those thoughts and certainly not about the intelligence that wasn't in the brain! And yet those thoughts thought in him … Those were the moments when Els realized that he was completely locked inside himself. He then fought with those unwanted emerging thoughts and tried to refute them within himself.

But the more he tried, the stronger they became. Then he simply tried to ignore the thoughts, but then they seemed to get stronger as well. In the meantime he revealed nothing of all this, and refused to say anything about it. But inwardly the conversation was all the more intense.

It would pass once he was back home and he would have to work very hard in preparation for his new position. After all, 'an empty mind is the devil's workshop'! Although he did not believe in any god or devil, he did find it strange that these unwanted thoughts arose more strongly the less he wanted them.

Els meanwhile was thinking: how do I get in touch with that man down there? I need to talk to him, or rather, Raymond needs to talk to him before we leave here. How do I throw that into the pot? Maybe she could write to him online? In the rationed digital access time they'd given themselves, she'd better look up the e-mail address of that centre down there and send him an e-mail. Or maybe his e-mail address was also on his card … Where did that go? Probably Raymond just threw it away.

On the other hand, she didn't want to do anything without him. They were always sincere and honest with each other, this would be a punch below-the-belt … She couldn't do that either. And she knew: if I suggested it, it would be rejected immediately.

It was a beautiful day in May and the future couple took a walk through the mountains and valleys to a hotel at a higher elevation. It could be reached by car, but you could also walk - and the walk was described as nice and not too difficult, albeit a long one. They could have a meal there and then possibly take a taxi back home — or the post car.

Gradually, more and more tourists had been coming to the area. It was clearly no longer what it used to be, but the area still attracted walkers in the summer and spring. So, they weren't surprised to see a bunch of cars parked there once they got to the hotel and discovered that the dining room was filled except for one small table.

"It's lovely here," said Raymond happily. "Look at that view! And to think that you could fill the whole space you see out there with intelligence — and some of it is already invisibly filled with intelligence!"

"Whatever," Els said. She didn't fancy this subject anymore!

They waited for the waitress to ask if there was a table for two left. Raymond turned around to look at the room and almost had a cardiac arrest in fright. There, at the window, in lively conversation, the man and his wife were sitting! Els had not seen them yet, and he said to her:

"I don't feel well, Els! Let's go, then we'll call a taxi outside!"

She looked at him and saw that he was pale. Simultaneously, she saw the man coming towards them. Raymond saw it too. There was no escape.

"What a surprise to see both of you here," the man said. "I wanted so much to talk to you, but I had no idea where to look for you. If you don't know someone's name, it's pretty much impossible … But look at this! They are just standing here! Can I invite you to join us at our table - we are still to order - so we can get to know each other over dinner?"

The colour had returned to Raymond's face and although he would have preferred to leave, he felt that this would be really rude. That, he wasn't. So, he said with a friendly smile:

"Thank you for your invitation, we'll be happy to accept, won't we, Els?"

Els was speechless. Her fervent wish had come true! She hadn't prayed because she didn't believe in any god — but she found it hard to imagine that it was a coincidence …

They shook hands at the table and sat down. Raymond facing the man, Els facing the woman …

The man said, seemingly perfectly relaxed:

"You may have noticed that I really saw you, those two evenings. Anyone who gives lectures, talks, is familiar with this phenomenon. There are always certain people in the audience who you really 'see', the others are more of a generality. But here and there someone catches the eye. That was the case with you twice, and I do wonder afterwards - I always do - what was the reason for that? In this case I had no answer. It was just that I felt very sorry that I did not speak with you! And it is clear: if good providence had not brought us together now, we would never have seen each other again …"

"You could always run into each other somewhere," Raymond mumbled vaguely. He felt like a rookie compared to this tyrant. The man gave the impression of being an Old Testament prophet or something like that. A great figure, filled with wisdom and - he thought - also with love. Again, those weird thoughts! What did he know about Old Testament prophets! Enough, apparently, to sense something similar in this man.

"Tell me," said the man, "are you here on holiday?"

Raymond nodded and didn't say a word. Els took up the conversation and said:

" Yes, we're in this area for four weeks. Unfortunately, two have already passed … We took a long holiday because he" - she nodded to Raymond – "has just been appointed as a professor in Amsterdam and before that whole procedure gets started we wanted to retreat into nature together for a few weeks."

"You are still young," said the man, "you must be a brilliant scientist to be nominated as a professor at such a young age. In what subject?"

"Human sciences and artificial intelligence … " Raymond grumbled. What was that man interfering for? He didn't feel like telling him any of this. But of course he was proud of it, so in some way he liked to talk about it …

"Interesting!" the man said and it wasn't just a cliche. "From what area of expertise are you going to do this?"

96

"I've studied artificial intelligence, nanotechnology, technical micro-biology and philosophy."

"For goodness' sake!" said the man.

"But tell me," Raymond asked, "what kind of background do you have?"

Els held her breath as she thought it sounded rather cheeky ... But the man was absolutely impassive and said:

"I've had a most remarkable career - I was a professor at a very young age, too."

Raymond's mouth fell open.

"Not as young as you: I was forty. In internal medicine - I did that for years. Then I took a different direction and now I've been here for many, many years. At the time when I held that post, the professor was something completely different than he or she is now. We were real bosses, head of the department, with a lot to contribute."

"Did you leave because it was going to change?" Raymond asked.

"No, it was already different, had been for a long time. No, why I left ... that's a long story, not so suitable for a first conversation over lunch."

Now Els recognised where she knew him from: she'd seen his picture at the clinic: one of the former professors.

"My profession was very concrete," the man said. "I can't really im-agine much about the scope of your teaching. What does a highly ed-ucated gentleman do when he has to teach arts and humanities, social sciences, and artificial intelligence?"

Because his vanity was being massaged, he thawed gently, uninten-tionally opening the door of that secret locker with its hidden thoughts ...

Raymond was seized by a profound sympathy for this man. He didn't notice it that way, because in his conscious thoughts he was engaged in a struggle with the same man. But below the surface he had a sense of great respect and a feeling that he had missed such a man as a father. This man radiated such certainty, such a consciousness of being above the daily struggle with things, that people wanted to let themselves be illumined by his sun ...

Raymond felt like he was just a little man in comparison, as some-one who also thought he knew something. And while in his conscious thoughts he was utterly convinced that he was right, beneath it lay a whole world of uncertainty. In that world also stood that locked cupboard with strange, almost spiritual-philosophical thoughts. He had decided not to look at them anymore, but they had repeatedly kept occurring to him.

Now the creator of such thoughts was sitting opposite him and he was given the opportunity to say what he wanted to say to this man.

"You have spoken," he said, "of man's ability to know how and what he thinks, to acquire an awareness of the technique of thought. Isn't that so?"

The man nodded. Els was shrivelling up inside … She thought: Don't say anything! But he carried on talking, and said:

"Science has made great progress in this field. We have now reached the point where we understand much of the activity of the brain. We see that part of the topography of the brain works digitally, i.e. on or off. Effective or not. Exactly like a computer. But still there is a big difference between the human brain and the computer and that big difference lies in the ability of the brain to perform an almost infinite number of computational processes at the same time, while the computer can only do that in the course of time. This means that the brain still surpasses the computer in the fullest sense, no matter how awkward the processes often are. But we are working hard on the possibility of analogue, simultaneous calculations of the same problem. Programming in DNA molecules seems to be one possibility. The brain remains the exemplar, but when technology is capable of making a computer perform an infinite number of computational processes at the same time, that computer will work infinitely better than the human brain, because of course it will eliminate an error percentage, which simply is there in the brain."

Els saw that it was nothing new to him at all. She saw that he was fully aware of all these scientific findings! Only Raymond, in the blaze of his own thoughts, was blind to this and did not realize that he was talking to someone who already knew all this, and had already established his point of view. That position was also determined by the fact that as a doctor he had a completely different view on physical functioning from a computer expert. Although Raymond would never admit that a doctor might have a better view on it. Els had the feeling that she was in cardiac arrest and that her breathing was no longer functioning. She looked across the table and just wanted them to be sitting opposite each other so they could start a conversation, and she wouldn't have to hear Raymond making a fool of himself.

But the man was far too courteous and gallant to let Raymond dig a hole for himself. He asked with interest where these investigations were taking place and where the results were published and, of course, Raymond was able to give the answers to all these questions flawlessly. When Raymond was finished he said:

"You know, I read a lot and I'm quite familiar with these investigations regarding the brain's thinking functions. But I have to admit, I'm neither a technician nor a neurophysiologist, so in a way I remain an amateur in that area and can't quite follow word for word what's being said about these things. But I don't think that is necessary either, in order to form a well-founded opinion about this research that is in progress and will certainly produce a lot of results. When I talk about the science of thinking and you talk about the science of thinking, the words may be the same, but the subject is really completely different. So you can't actually say that you would want to trade one for the other, or that you could refute the one with the other. They are not two theories that can compete with each other, because they are really about completely different things. I think it's important to establish that. It's a different subject."

Raymond had the feeling that his weapons were being knocked out of his hands and that he suddenly didn't know what he was actually fighting against anymore. If it was something completely different, then both visions could possibly coexist. He said:

"Then why, listening to your speech, did I get the impression that we're talking about the same thing, but that our visions are completely different?"

"That has to do," said the man, "with the fact that the words are the same and that you could get lost in the meaning. But the theme is really a different one. I would never claim that the studies in neurophysiology and technology are nonsense, or that none of them are accurate. Of course, the brain in the human body is the organ that has to do with thinking. That you can determine the relationship between thinking and the special structure of the brain, I would never dispute. I don't think I did that in my two lectures, either. But indeed, it is true that all scientific inventions have to be *interpreted* as well, and things can go terribly wrong there. After all, certain hypotheses are assumed, confirmed or denied by research, and there always remains a large percentage that must be shown to be incorrect later on. You see a certain primitiveness in the functioning and structure of the brain. Of course, this primitive quality also lies in the way we form hypotheses in science. The search for connections and explanations requires a good degree of interpretation, and you know as well as I do, that this is not always so robustly constructed."

"That's why," Raymond said, "there will be such a revolution in human scientific ability in the future. When that personality-dependent interpretation will have been completely replaced by a standardized interpretation with the computer!"

"Yet then," said the man, "you forget that it is still man's weak interpretative skills that underlie the computer software."

"Sure!" said Raymond. "But just as the brain is capable of self-regulation and self-improvement, so in computer technology we are gradually developing the possibility of self-regulation, self-correction and self-development. Once a mistake has been made, the future computer will learn from it and will no longer make that mistake again. While the tendency for misinterpretation in a human being is not so easily overcome."

"I completely agree with you, that this could not be overcome so easily in a human being, and that is why I don't yet have such a great future for artificial intelligence in mind."

"I don't think you understand the self-learning principle?"

"I do," said the man, "but at the same time I see that the fallibility of the man who makes the computer, lives on in the device. Apparently, that escapes you. But when you really get involved in these processes, you have to experience that in the long run, don't you? I use the dictaphone a lot. When dictating patients' letters of discharge in the old days, there used to be a secretary who would listen to the text on the tape and then type it up. Nowadays, when I want to make a note, I speak that note and the equipment writes it out in a document. That's a splendid technical improvement - that speech can be recognised in such a way that it is converted into written language! When I then take a look at the piece of text that has been written out, a number of fundamental mistakes do of course stand out. These errors show very clearly that the speech recognition system does not understand what it is transposing. It is a kind of genius photography of sound. But even if you say a certain name a hundred times, the system, even if you have improved it a hundred times, corrupts that name every time. I think you could improve that by improving the capture. But it's also clear that the system doesn't read correlations. It doesn't know when something is an article or a stand-alone word, a conjunction, a verb, or whatever. I am very grateful for that system, it saves us an incredible amount of writing. But it also shows very clearly how that conversion from speech to text comes about."

Raymond said:

"Surely you can understand that it's only a matter of time before we get to the point where what you're speaking is recognized as a pattern, that from those patterns it is converted into text?"

"I believe that," said the man, "but even then, you'll see that the device follows the patterns without realising it. And I believe that that's where the separation lies between the technique of thinking as you see it and the technique of thinking I'm talking about. That's why they are two different areas, and they shouldn't conflict with each other. If they're not wrongly confused with each other, they can coexist."

Raymond, with his 'big mouth', was completely overwhelmed. Was it true, what this man was saying? If it were really true that you could see in a speech recognition system that the device doesn't understand a word of what it's transposing … How did this man see that? He had used that software himself and he didn't notice it at all. He found it extraordinarily fascinating how what he had recorded was not infallible, but still usable in text. Maybe he needed to look more closely at where the system failed rather than at where it worked well?

Els got involved in the conversation and talked about the Preludes and Fugues by Bach that Raymond had played and in which she had identified which was synthetic.

"That must be in the same area," she said, "as what you are talking about with regard to speech recognition. Something is being ignored because it can't be caught in a system and that 'something' that is being ignored, that's exactly what you were talking about in your lecture."

Eva hadn't spoken a word yet, but now she intervened:

"Is that really true? Are there any synthetic Bach Preludes and Fugues!?"

Els nodded and replied:

"Yes, composed by the computer with pattern recognition."

The conversation flowed off, as it were, into a number of innocent babbling mountain streams; a dangerous waterfall was not to be feared along these meanderings.

Raymond was given the opportunity to nurse his wounds and recover, and asked:

"Maybe you'd like to tell me over lunch what thinking you are talking about?"

The food was served and the man said:

"I'd love to, but let's eat this delicious food before it gets cold! I would like to suggest that we set aside the formal Mr. and Mrs. My name is Johannes."

"Eva, Raymond, Els … " they said one by one.

While enjoying the tasty food – consciousness of which was rather obscured by other strong impressions - Els was thinking: We've had the First Act now, soon we'll have the Second Act and that will probably present a completely different view of the whole thing … Or maybe this will be the second part of the game, the part that will be decisive. She felt a bit nervous about it. At the same time, she could see that Raymond was not really comfortable.

He wasn't on the warpath, she knew him well enough to know that he wasn't in a mood for heavy discussion. He was probably impressed, just as she was, by the impact this man had on you.

Indeed, Raymond cleared his plate, deeply impressed by the man opposite him. A thought swirled through him: Isn't the one who is speaking greater proof of the truth of his words, than the words themselves? He couldn't be harbouring a thought like that just now! But one thought after another of that nature stirred up like dust being whipped up in his consciousness. This man had been a professor for years, he must have been very skilled, and Raymond thought: I will never be able to achieve such comprehensive learning. I'll have to think about that question later, as to why I wouldn't.

And so with him too, tasting the delicious food was pushed into the background by disturbing thoughts.

In the meantime, Eva was talking about her husband … She was saying:

"I got to know him when he first got here, I had been coming here for a few years. We sat next to each other in the room and he said he was a professor, precisely where I was going to do my internships after my holiday. He was struck by the theme of the lecture we were listening to and he was left somewhat distraught. Outside, the master said to me, 'Go and see, girl, how he is doing?'"

"A master?" Els asked.

"Yes, that's our Buddhist teacher who originally founded this centre. Well, that's how we got to know each other and what Johannes says is true: in those days a professor was still quite a leader with great author-ity - and he was the crowning glory in that respect! I never met anyone who knew and could do as much as he did. And I still haven't. Believe me, Raymond, if you enter into a discussion with him about the sub-ject you were talking about, you will find out that he knows everything about it. He does say very modestly that he's an amateur, but I'm afraid you're going to discover that he knows all those details that you know like a master. I'm just telling you, it's not that easy with him!"

Johannes laughed and said:

"I didn't intend to pose here as the authoritarian professor of the past. I'm very interested, because there's a professional here opposite me, and I wouldn't say that I know all that better - although I have read a lot about it and, as I said, have taken a stand on it."

It gave Raymond goose bumps and made him very annoyed that he felt so much respect for this man, without being able to feel respect for his train of thought. That was the wrong way round, he thought. That's why he decided to follow his train of thought very closely and, where possible, refute it lucidly.

Between the main course and the dessert, Johannes leaned back some-what in his chair and said:

"I'll try to answer your question now - although it's a question that I have been answering in lectures for decades and I can't quite imagine how I could make it clear what it's all about in a quarter of an hour or so. But it was about the question: What, then, is the thinking I am talk-ing about? I could explain that in a more spiritual context, but I think you wouldn't be able to handle that very well, because you would have to start from certain assumptions that you can't make. I have a quote from a great predecessor of yours, who was more or less at the cradle of modern computer technology, but who, as he was, still had a differentiated view of the one thinking and the other thinking. So, I will read that quote to you first and then I will try to explain it to you."

For a moment Raymond thought, does he know that quote by heart? But Johannes took his iPhone out of his pocket, looked it up, and said:

"I've got it!" and started reading it:

" 'But what if these theories really were true and we, miraculously, had shrunk and ended up in the brain of a thinking person? We would see all the pumps, pistons, gears and levers working, and we could fully describe how they work, as far as mechanics are concerned, and we could also fully describe the thinking processes of the brain. But in this description, thinking would not be mentioned at all! It would be nothing more than a description of pumps, pistons, and levers!'[3]

It was, of course, clear what this scholar from the beginning of the scientific era wanted to say: You can gain so much knowledge about the human brain and its functioning during thinking, but you have not known thinking itself."

Raymond nodded and said:

"I understand. At least I understand what this man wrote. But if that's true, that's what it's all about, of course."

"Sure," said Johannes, "that's what it's all about…. You said earlier that the mapping of the topography and the function of the brain is in full swing and that they have certainly achieved results. I am familiar with these statements, but when you look for the articles about them and start reading them - and you will have done so anyway - you discover as I said earlier what is very questionable here: namely, the interpretation. In fact, it has not yet been possible to make a direct determination of the functions of the central nervous system. They are always indirect conclusions. Between the observation on which the conclusion rests and the conclusion lies that familiar field of interpretation. One creates the impression that there is a certainty there, but you know as well as I do, that that is not the case at all. Furthermore, the direct examination of the brain, which is somewhat reliable, is only possible when one has

---

[3] 'G.W. Leibnitz (1646 - 1716)

direct access to the brain and that is only possible with an opened skull. So the examination is not carried out on humans but on mice, for example. This is based on the assumption that a mouse only has a more primitive set of brains than humans, not a totally different one. That's an interpretation. It could very well be that a human does not descend in a straight line from an animal, but is a species on its own, where the same kind of leap in development can be seen as between the mineral and the plant, the plant and the animal, the animals and people, then, in this case. You could say that you can go even further and then you would say: the next step in creation is the transition from the human being to the angel, where you wouldn't say that this angel is a result of the human being. Rather you would say: "man is a result of the angels."

"That's an area," Raymond said, " that consists entirely of assumptions and interpretations."

"Yes, I'm not saying you have to take this for true. I just want to give it as a thought: that the theory of evolution has been interpreted in such a way that there is a gradual transition between the four natural kingdoms. I want to say, that's an interpretation and not an actual observation."

"I'd have to delve deeper into that," Raymond said. "I don't have a direct response to that. But, of course, that gradual line of evolution is the generally accepted scientific theory."

"Yes," said Johannes, "attend to your words: you're using the word 'theory' ".

"But supported by evidence."

"Maybe it's possible to provide other evidence as well that will shake up this theory but, as I said, it will take us a few decades to work through that with each other. A quarter of an hour between the main course and the dessert is too short for that! I just want to make my point very clear - that the research into the thinking of the brain, on which you base your entire vision, is a very shaky whole, that it depends on interpretations. Hypothesis and interpretation of the result - and as a thinker you really shouldn't be satisfied with that."

"We have nothing else - and we can expect the hypothesis and interpretation of research results to become better and finer, especially now that the computer is helping us!"

"I must once again point out that the computer has been programmed on the basis of existing hypotheses and interpretations. You cannot cure a disease with the disease itself. Homeopathy is something else, you cure the disease with something that resembles it. But a cure with the disease itself – you do see that you can't do that, don't you?"

"Now you still haven't said which thinking it is that you are talking about!"

"I hesitate a little bit about that, too," said Johannes. "Because it seems to me that every thought we form is now vitally important to the life of your vision … "

"Speak freely … " said Raymond. "The authority with which you do that, the self-confidence in your train of thought, the meticulousness with which you choose your words, give me reason enough to take everything you say seriously."

"I'm glad to hear that!" said Johannes. " Well … Just as the computer is constructed thanks to the scientifically coherent thoughts of the scientific technicians, of the people who develop this computer, so there is also a thought underlying the human being himself. That's what I'm talking about. Not the thinking that is developed in life on the basis of outer details, but the thinking that was there before Man. To evolve, why would the computer need people? Because it couldn't be designed meaningfully in any other way. How then is it possible that the whole scientific thinking, the educated collective of men and women in this world can believe that this wonderful creature 'mankind' came into being by itself?"

"That's simply the theory of creationism!" said Raymond.

"No, that's too quick a dismissal! Of course, the next step is to say: there must be a creative being that Man himself has thought up. I didn't want to go that far, I wanted to say that the thought 'Man' must have been there before Man himself. Just as the computer functions in ever better and more perfect ways through time and thanks to the thinking of the scientific technicians, so the human being also goes through an evolution. But not from below as it were, from nature alone, but from above. That is what I am talking about."

"But that's based on an assumption!"

"What do you think you are talking about? That is also based on an assumption, because you assume that what is very difficult to find as a function of the brain through hypothesis, interpretation of research facts and new hypotheses, is the science of thinking. You can still - I suppose - conclude the actual presence of thoughts, but that their origin lies in the brain, that is just as much an assumption as my thesis that thinking precedes Man."

"Then both of us seem to be thinking in a somewhat indefinite way…"

Johannes laughed and said:

"No, you are, of course, not me!"

Raymond started to feel angry, but he swallowed it and waited.

"What would you say," said Johannes, "if that thinking, which precedes Man, could be found in yourself as the source of your intelligence?"

"That would be wonderful! But that's exactly what we are doing in science!"

"No, no … Think along with me: you have to let go of your own vision and try to follow what I'm saying."

"I'm doing my best … " Raymond grumbled.

Smiling, Johannes said:

"Imagine that somewhere inside you there is the source where you as a human being have been thought. Those wouldn't be technical thoughts, because they weren't there at all. They wouldn't be physical thoughts either, because the body wasn't there yet. It would have to be a thought world in which everything is contained, but which would only be realized in the actual forming of the human being. If you could go back to that point within yourself, without equipment, without the help of scientists, but directly, no doubt, then you would find a point where the wisdom of Man, the wisdom that has made Man, and the wisdom that can be found in Man, would originate."

He looked directly at Johannes and said:

"It is, indeed, a wonderful idea. But if it is a world of thought that has preceded Man – and apparently is still at work in Man - then you cannot reach it with the physical scientific method. That means that you are on slippery ground with research into it. You move in a certain direction and there is nothing to show you that what you think is wrong. Thus, for me, this whole train of thought you have developed in those two lectures and also here at the table is - I don't want to say 'worthless', as I think it is very beautiful and also in fact consistent in itself - still completely useless from a scientific point of view."

It was clear that Johannes was not impressed. He was accustomed to such contradiction, and at this moment he chose not to react to it. He said:

"From your point of view, I can understand your reaction very well and, in a way, it's justified. If you would like to get to know the scientific nature of the thinking I am talking about, and also the scientific nature of the research we are doing into it, then you would have to get into it much more deeply. And I gather that that is not interesting for you."

"Excuse me!" said Raymond. "I do find it interesting, but I'm finding it, literally, coming 'out of the blue' and I don't want to get involved with that."

Raymond felt an enormous power surging into him and, carried by that power, he declared:

"You're talking about the shaky foundation of the brain's reverse engineering. You come up with the right arguments for this, but in fact you have left the engineering side out of the equation. And for us, that is the confirmation time and time again that our research results are based on reality. I have not only read about it, I have also been active in research and would like to remain active. I was in America for a while, and after that I worked for a number of years in Lausanne on my dissertation and did a sort of internship with the great promoter of this research in Europe. There I learned an incredible amount, but also saw a lot. Although they are minuscule steps that are apparently taken, it is true that what is found to be so minuscule in terms of brain activity can really be seen at the level of the cell. In a suitable computer these processes are simulated and when this simulation has the same effect as the observed reality in the brain itself, then you have retrospectively proven that your hypotheses and your assumptions and your interpretations have been correct."

Johannes looked back and said:

"I've already told you, of course, I don't reject the scientific side of this brain research. What I must reject, however, is the isolation of thought as a *product* of the brain. That's what you're concerned with, isn't it? Determining how thinking is produced in the brain. While I know myself that thinking is there beforehand, and the brain reacts to it. That will be very difficult to prove scientifically, especially when the researcher is not willing to include this hypothesis in his research."

108

"How can you," Raymond said, "assume something that is totally imperceptible as a cause for something that then becomes perceptible?"

"Well," said Johannes, "that is in fact the case with all the plans, goals, constructions and architecture, for example. Something is first thought up, and then it comes into reality and only becomes visible there. So, you can appreciate already that it is not so strange, this process."

Raymond said:

"The plans, the construction drawings, the goals et cetera, of course, are always borrowed from the visible."

"What about Bach's music?" Johannes responded. "A part of it may have resulted from what was customary at the time, but with Bach it is, of course, precisely the special thing that he adds to it, which makes it specifically Bach's music. It had previously lived in him invisibly, and following his life we can also hear it … "

Raymond did not have a direct answer to that, although he felt that the comparison was not entirely correct, after all.

He said:

"But look, Johannes, thousands of highly educated scientists around the world are working on this fathoming of the brain and, hopefully, eventually consciousness. You know as well as I do, as a matter of fact, that a lot of work is being done on this."

"Yes," said Johannes, "and also that a lot of money is being spent on it!"

"Exactly!" Raymond said. "But how are you going to make it clear to me that what you want to develop down here in this centre with a just few people, based on a vague idea, and with a limited number of listeners, how is that ever going to outweigh this great global project of fathoming the human brain? Do you know that this is a project in which all university and technical institutes are working together? That they are sharing their information - it's not a personal matter of honour, but it's really a global activity - and we can expect multiple benefits for medicine as well?"

"Again," Johannes said, "I don't reject that aspect. But if you ask me: How would you like to put this out into the world with just a few people here, based on a vague idea and a handful of listeners? Then I can only answer that you apparently have no idea about the power of the active mind: a human being who carries that power within him has more effect than, let me say, a thousand scientists or, maybe even, ten thousand scientists!"

"That's arrogance!"

"Arrogance is when you convince yourself of something - that just isn't so. I tell you, there is another origin of thinking - the very origin of thinking - and it can only be found by every human being for himself. While you are in the process of developing an intelligence that will supposedly be available to everyone equally, we are in the process of finding the origin of human intelligence. That is an absolutely individual free-thinking process. Anyone who wants to can participate, but anyone who participates will have to do it within themselves. That makes it unattractive. You'd all rather sit in a large room at the screen and let the computer do the thinking for you!"

"But you still have to do some thinking for yourself, don't you!"

"We, this handful of thinkers you have seen here, have nothing external that can be given away. There is no possibility to be helpful in some outward way. You really have to want to take every step yourself. But you will agree with me that only in that way there is true freedom!? No one on the outside can make you do anything. You can tell from our conversation here: I may try to convince you with my arguments. If you yourself, from your own volition and understanding, can't reach the conclusion that there is something in what Johannes says, then it's best to leave: you go your way, you forget about Johannes - and that is your freedom, too. There is nothing or no one who can bring you to anything but your own insight. It is not my discoveries that you must follow. It is my discoveries that you are allowed to use to explore, test and make your own. But that's quite an assignment. I have been a scientist myself and I can say that I have made a great effort to make all the details of internal medicine my own. That was quite a task and I haven't stopped doing it, even now - I want to keep abreast of developments. But the effort it requires is nothing compared to what you have to do within yourself to grasp that human thought that preceded your existence. Once you have grasped that, it becomes possible to see your life of action, your will, in a different light. You will see that this is in fact an activity in the human being that has yet to blossom fully.

"These are the two poles that you can discover in your inner life and that will lead you to the realisation of what a human being actually is,

110

and then to identify who you really are. For us, that is the most beautiful fruit of being human, and we will do everything we can to make it permeate the world - however difficult that may be, for the army of scientists - to which you, too, belong - is strong and powerful. You have the physical, the mechanical, the electrical, the magnetic, the different forces of nature at hand and we have to try to operate outside those fields. So yes, we're having a very, very difficult time!"

Raymond was again somewhat impressed by these words and he asked:

"Is there a religious aspect to this "science," shall I say?"

"Certainly," said Johannes, "but not any existing church. The next step is to think of a being who has had this thought. That being then also should have had the whole environment, all processes, all tissues, all nuclei, electrons, all planets, black holes, galaxies et cetera in his mind. What you are hoping for – I am very familiar with this, that you hope that one day you will be able to encompass the entire cosmos with artificial intelligence - that is an image, a counter-image, to what is actually already the case. The macrocosm and the microcosm, the whole of the universe is filled with intelligence, and we as humans have been given the ability to gradually empathize through our tiny intellect in that enormous intelligent world. But what do we do? We invent a device that can mimic a little bit in miniature what we ourselves do at a bigger scale, and what is infinitely greater in the cosmos - and think that such a device must then eventually replace all human and superhuman thinking, hiding it away under the power of that device!"

"Well," Raymond said, "if you look at it that way, I've either pledged my heart to the devil or signed a contract with him with my blood … . But there's no way I can see it that way!"

"I can understand that very well … " said Johannes, "you have been accustomed from an early age to the scientific thoughts that are now yours. And then some strange man comes along and says it's different. Of course, you can't accept that!"

This collided with Raymond's vanity. He never wanted to boast of his giftedness and always behaved modestly with it. In the depths, of course, there was a great pride in his intelligence. Now this fellow here has told him that he is stuck in a certain pattern of thought and that he can't just escape it! That clashed with his vanity. Wasn't he capable of anything that had to do with intelligence? Couldn't he also take a step into the unknown and stay there for a while to experience if there was something worthwhile there?

There was a silence. They were all so quiet because the battle had taken their breath away. This was not just a conversation between Johannes and Raymond, this was of world importance. In a hotel somewhere on a mountain, two men were sitting opposite each other, one older and one younger. The older one represented the spiritual dignity of Man in an all-encompassing greatness of thought; and the other looked to the science of the smallest details, and expected from knowing how the smallest elements work to come up with a technical method to produce the greatest thoughts.

One was thoroughly filled with the moral implications of his task, while the other asked no moral questions at all. It was the technical world he was engaged in. He was a scientist and an engineer at the same time, and he felt no limits to the consequences of his work. Now he felt challenged, described as someone who wouldn't be able to follow a line of thought that wasn't his own.

"Good Johannes," he said, "you've caught me! You've grabbed that part of me that I'm most proud of, because I feel hurt. But, precisely because of that hurt, I also feel that I have to show you that I can really elevate myself to these thoughts of yours. After all, a man can do what he wants and up to now I haven't wanted to do that. But now that you're saying: 'You can't!', naturally, I have to say: 'I'll just show you what I can do!' "

The other three burst out laughing, and the tension drained away.

"You may laugh about it," he said, "but it is rather serious for me! I'll be honest, Johannes: I don't believe a word of what you're saying but, of course, I am capable of delving into thoughts I don't myself believe. After all, that's what you have to do in the study."

"The problem," said Johannes, "is that this is not just about going deeper into thoughts; it is also about a certain thinking technique. You can't discover with your ordinary mode of studying whether what I'm saying is true. You have to do just as much research for that as you do in your outer career. So, you would have to be prepared to undertake certain exercises, to strengthen your thinking in such a way that it becomes possible to do research into that as well. Otherwise it would be far too ephemeral … "

Again, Raymond got goose bumps. It was like a fairy tale, in which he allowed himself to be challenged to accept a task, which would take a lot of work. He foresaw that, but he said:

"In view of my future position, it's also interesting, of course, to immerse myself in your train of thought. My academic task is: the implications of artificial intelligence for the human sciences - and I think it would be good to include the possibility that there is a separate world of thought. Because that's what you mean, isn't it?"

"That's what I'm talking about, yes." Johannes said.

"We've got a fortnight left." Raymond said. "So how do we go about that?"

"Let's hope we've got a lot more than a fortnight. But that should be enough for a first introduction! It's not that busy here yet, I can free up an hour and a half per day. Then we'll systematically build up access to the thinking I'm talking about. I don't know whether we'll have to do this every day or whether we'll have to do it every other day, I'll have to take a look – then I will ask one of the others to describe his, let's say, field of work with us. I think it's a good thing that Els is coming with you, so that you can get to know this process together."

"Isn't that a little too much honour for us?" Raymond asked.

"Do you think it's too much yourself, an hour and a half per day?"

"No, no, but if you had to do that with every passer-by … "

"You, my dear Raymond, are simply not 'every passer-by'! So, if you think this is a good plan, we'll carry it out over the next few days."

"I'm very honoured … What time do you have in mind?"

"Same time every day: 10 o'clock seems like a good time."

"We'll be there!"

They were taken home by Johannes and Eva and a little later they sat, slightly bewildered, back in their room. Els said:

"The room is exactly the same as it was before this meeting … But do you feel that, too: that nothing is the same anymore?"

Raymond nodded and said slowly:

"You're right, Els. Nothing is the same anymore; and it seems as if even the tables and chairs are aware of it…"

For the third time, the next morning they drove down the hill, parked the car and went into the hall, this time not to attend a lecture, but for a special appointment with the 'chief' himself. They went to the desk, where an assistant asked if she could help them. Raymond said:

"We have an appointment with Johannes Leven."

The girl looked at him in surprise, then looked at the appointment list and said:

"Indeed, I'll take you to his room."

She went ahead of them, into a long corridor, knocked on a certain door and opened it on the signal: "Yes, come in!"

Raymond let Els lead the way. There he was sitting at his desk, got up immediately, the chief of this dubious institute, but so impressive that your dubiety was soon swept away. The windows in the room offered a view of distant mountains. Johannes invited them not to sit at the desk, but by the window, so that they were not disturbed by the lamp.

"Are you sticking to your decision, Raymond?" Johannes asked before he sat down.

"Yes!" Raymond said almost solemnly.

"And Els, how is your position on this?"

"I haven't agreed with Raymond at all from the beginning, I am actually shocked by the fact that he is so firmly convinced of something that, as far as I am concerned, is not human, that I am just intensely grateful that we have come here, have met you and are now going to get some private instruction from you!"

Johannes laughed and said:

"Okay, then I'll join you. I will have to give you both a little private lecture before we can really get to work. Because the kind of thinking I'm talking about is of course not as fact-based as the brain with the neurons, dendrites, synapses, the operation of certain neurotransmitters, and so on. That research is difficult enough and also rather elusive, I know that," he said, "but at least you have an actually tangible field of research. When you start looking for this other way of thinking, you

115

have to do without that, and in actuality you have to make the research field visible first. That's where the difficulty lies. That's why it's an area of research that's not taken seriously, because it's not obvious. Man's thinking is an ethereal, transparent, elusive whole. As soon as you focus your gaze on it, it is already gone and you have to make an effort to remember what you were thinking. Taking notes to some extent captures what previously occurred to you in such a transient way. We always have a longing to have everything we want to explore outside of us, as something concrete, something dense, something material, upon which you can let the eye fall - even if it is through a microscope or through indirect observation. That's not what I'm talking about. Although thinking is constantly unfolding within us, we do not have it in mind and it escapes our perception as if it were mercury. You know, as soon as you want to capture mercury, it jumps away! It's the same with thinking. In fact, you can do nothing other than set it in motion again and again, consciously with a subject of your own choice or a subject that you get from me, for example. And then try to investigate what you want to investigate. And, at the same time, make what you produce so stable that it becomes a perceptible field of research."

"May I ask questions?" Raymond said.

"For sure!"

"The question is, of course, why would you do that?"

"Naturally, there's a whole world of wisdom behind the motivation to do this. I suggest we talk about that in stages. There is one thing we agree on, Raymond, and that is that the time has come for mankind to take control of evolution itself. Only, in your view that will come about because a level of technological perfection will be found that can create a new kind of human; in my view - and this has a different background than the usual natural science – the way is that the human learns to grasp that part in himself, where he is in control, and then from there to take further control of evolution itself."

"Do you know the philosophy of Teilhard de Chardin?" Raymond asked.

"Of course!" said Johannes. "An interesting figure, who has also envisaged a turning point for mankind. But he falls into the trap of the visible, the measurable, the weighable - and finally into the trap of technology as the great covenant for mankind.

"So, by simply starting to think, we must bring the field of investigation into the light of consciousness. This means that you don't focus your thinking on a research set-up outside you, but you focus it on itself, just as it makes itself willing to be examined."

Raymond said:

"I am put in mind of the Baron of Münchhausen, who wanted to lift himself up with his own wig … !"

Johannes smiled and said:

"I can imagine. But still, when you really start to do this, you gradually begin to experience that it really is something other than that. You do have to set the thinking in motion yourself in order to contemplate it completely self-consciously; but in fact, of course, the thinking is not only active then. It is also a given.

"I want to ask you the following question: You, Raymond, have given much of your mind power, much of your intelligence to arithmetic. You are not so interested in logic as you find it in Aristotle, which you could use somehow as food for thought to create a research field. In your case, I would rather choose another field from the seven liberal arts, namely the basic concept of the universe that Pythagoras had in antiquity. In fact, you modern natural scientists see it that way, too. Arithmetic is basic in the universe. Only, you are talking about millions, billions, trillions, and more. You use complicated formulas to apply calculations. What was originally seen in antiquity as the basic concept of the universe, has completely disappeared from sight. That is: number itself. Until well into the Middle Ages, the art of dealing with numbers was still practised as a true science. That art was applied in geometry, in astronomy, also in music. The great medieval buildings like the gothic cathedrals were built on the principles of applied number. The fact that a cathedral is really built in a certain way, with dimensions and apparent proportions, that it is also structurally sound, is a kind of reverse engineering you could say. A simulation of the inner art of numbers."

"An interesting point of view!" Raymond said, sincerely.

"So you can't say that what first becomes public through Pythagoras and then works on through Plato into the Middle Ages, into the school of Chartres, for example, couldn't be described as an exact science. Now it is not the case that we are of the opinion that for evolution to continue, you have to go back to the old, because the old has to be reintroduced. We certainly do not see it that way, but when we think about what has become visible in the art of a Gothic cathedral, when we want to trace that, then we have to abandon the millions and the billions, the incalculable quantities of the formulas, that you can deduce with human thinking but blinds us to the coherence in the whole….. we have to go back to the simplicity of number - and I would therefore like to ask you to close your eyes and ask yourselves: what is actually: one?"

"What do you mean by: one?" Raymond asked.

"The number one: 1."

They closed their eyes and stepped into invisibility …

About five minutes later, Raymond said:

"In the first place, I can only concentrate for a moment. And in the second place, I really don't know what to do with 'one'. It just depends on which unit you associate it with. When I say 1 millimetre, that's something very different from 1 kilometre. They're both 1."

Els said:

"I do get an experience of some kind of uniformity, whether it's a millimetre or a kilometre, that doesn't really matter. It's about what you express with it."

"I don't get that!" said Raymond. "For me, numbers are always related to something, and that's why a number is relative. When I say 1 millimetre, I've got 1,000 in a metre."

"So," said Johannes, " you will have to abstract from the millimetre, the metre, kilometre …   … and try to think of the 'one' in itself."

"But what you said will happen …   My thoughts fly away from me like balls of mercury as soon as I try to hold them!"

"That's a matter of practice," said Johannes. " You will see, if you do it a second, third, fourth time, it will be better already. Now: try to think of 1, abstracted from what you want to express with it - not a millimetre, not a gram, not a second, just 1."

After about five minutes Raymond said:

"Then I've got nothing at all. I don't know what 1 in itself is. I do know what a relative is, as I said, but 1 detached from all unity, 1 in itself, that's totally meaningless to me."

"How can you say that!" Els said. "1 means undivided, doesn't it?"

"But you can really divide 1 up!"

"No, even that you can't, because if you divide 1, it's not a whole number anymore. I think that is what we are really doing, isn't it? So, 1 is undivided, not divisible. It is fascinating, almost shocking, when you realize that in the world of numbers there is a principle that stands for undividedness!"

"Well … " said Raymond. "Then I'll have to try again."

"I'm improving indeed," he said. "1 then becomes for me a point, without dimension, no extension, not nothing, but a point. I don't have a meaning for that. Surely you could become quite alarmed about that if you become aware that you have been working with units for - let's say - thirty years and that you don't know what 1 actually represents! It's a tool, you might say, and you use it as it suits you. But what it is exactly - that seems pretty nonsensical to wonder about … "

Johannes said:

"It can help you further, when, in your search for the meaning of 1, you become aware that you have no meaning. After all, holding on to not having a meaning leads to finding the meaning. Because there is meaning, of course. It is not just an abstract little thing where we can turn it into billions, and with formulas perform the most complicated conjuring tricks. When humanity was still 'stupid' and did not look any further into numbers than he could keep in mind, there still was an awareness of what 1 actually is: 1 detached from all objects, from all units. Of all measures and weights: 1 as 1."

"It's very hard for me just to look at that 1!" said Raymond. "I want to reason and I do. I'm starting to compare 1 with 0 and 2, with 1/2, with -1. But now you say, I have to get rid of that and I have to face the principle of 1."

"I don't understand why this is so difficult … " Els said.

Johannes said:

"You, as a doctor, haven't become so caught up in number. The path Raymond has taken is the path which is becoming more and more complicated in the handling of number, and the energy lies in that handling and no longer in what the number itself actually is. That's what I'm trying to lead him back to now."

"I'm beginning to understand what you mean, anyway," Raymond said. "And I also believe that I will be able to focus on 1 as a number and stay with that for a while … "

"Let's go for a walk first!" Els said when they reached the car park. "Otherwise it will probably not come to that. I've found a pleasant walk that starts here and also finishes here. Then we can prepare for tomorrow, because we will need to."

Raymond laughed and said:

"Yes, this is going to be a crash course. But I like that … Come on, let's go for a nice walk!"

The mountain path was narrow and they had to proceed most of the way in single file. There was no opportunity to talk quietly about the experiences of the past hour. That was good, too. Those experiences were given the opportunity to penetrate well and to find a place in the being of both of them.

It was quite cloudy and rather chilly. It did them both good to have to put in a lot of physical effort. Raymond noticed how much effort it took him to stop his thoughts and open his senses widely, so that that majestic environment could really impress him. He actually felt very happy … Here he was, walking with Els, with the prospect of an interesting and challenging position, and as a preparation for this he was getting a glimpse of a completely different way of thinking – whose existence he did not as yet recognise, but which by now he suspected of existing, because the 'prophet' seemed to be a completely genuine human being.

When they returned to the house after a few hours, it seemed as if everything in it had taken on a different form again.

Raymond asked:

"How's our Internet ration? Do you want to maintain that?"

"Of course!" Els said surprised. "Why?"

"I feel an irresistible urge to search the internet for 1, unity. For Pythagoras and Plato … "

"You can do that in your ration time anyway," she said. "You'll just have to restrict yourself, and I think that's a good thing."

" Okay, okay … " he said and sat down with his laptop.

After half an hour he had got a comprehensive impression of what can be found on the internet about the number 1 from Pythagoras to Leibniz with the monad; the corpus hermeticum, neoplatonism, Jamblychus, Porphyrius, Aristotle, even Thomas Aquinas, and especially not to forget Boëthius. Names that were all familiar to him, from reviews of their work in his philosophy studies. He immediately saw that these thinkers had very specific statements and insights into what 1 is, but he didn't have the time to find it all out in detail. It had to remain a general impression, which could not be further differentiated. He felt that in a way it hurt his soul. He experienced his own nature, the way he had always studied, wanting to absorb everything that could be found about something as quickly as possible - preferably reaching conclusive results right away. That didn't seem to be working out now, and it seemed to fit the nature of the number 1 …

When his time was up he sat down with Els and said:
"I believe I must retreat into my thinking a few times before tomorrow and try to think through the meaning of this number 1, of the unity, as it were, hidden behind that figure."
"Yes, so do I! Do you think that tomorrow we will continue with the number 1, or would Johannes move on to the number 2?"
"I suspect that he would like to hear some of our results first and that tomorrow we will stay with the 1. I don't want to disappoint him and, more importantly, I don't want to disappoint myself, so that I can state what Pythagoras could do, what Plato could do, what Thomas Aquinas could do, what Aristotle could do and we'll see about that: 'Raymond can't do that!' "
Els was laughing.
"What's this, this urge in you to want to be able to do all that?"
"When I had to engage with Plato in my studies - I found him an interesting thinker, but of course rather vague, although there are certain dialogues where accuracy seems to be the main theme, as in the Timaeus. I chose that as the theme for my thesis, I believe in the first or second year, the Symposium of Plato: and so I came across the translation into Latin and Italian from the Renaissance by Marsilio Ficino. Marsilio Ficino also wrote a commentary and you can still get that book. It's called 'About Love'; I think I read it in English. It describes two aspects of love. For Plato, love is the desire for beauty. Philosophy is

the desire for wisdom, but love is the desire for beauty. These principles are discussed extensively in the Symposium from all sorts of angles. Ficino has given an explanation of this. I must say, I was really in a very elevated mood at the time because of that. I had actually forgotten about it a bit, but that was a period in my life where I completely let go of arithmetic and surrendered completely to the thoughts about love. Two pillars of love are presented: one is shame, which prevents you from having thoughts, feelings and actions you should be ashamed of; and the other is the desire for honour, for fame, for glory - but in a way that is just. That's where I found a kind of justification for my 'honour', my 'ambition'. That this is actually a high expression of love. Honour is seen as a bad quality and, of course, it can become so when it leads to jealousy, over-zealousness, competition. But when you keep that ambition to yourself, a lot comes about because of it. And that's what I feel right now: Johannes has challenged me, he has not hurt my honour in any way, but challenged me. Everyone would agree, when encountering this personality of Johannes, when a kind of ambition to want to emulate him arises. And then you can't really say anymore that what he's saying is nonsense."

"But that never occurred to me - to think he's talking rubbish!"

"No, not you, but me. If we hadn't run into him at the hotel, I'd have gone home with some kind of crude belief that it is all nonsense, what I've heard here. Now he has challenged me and I want to do everything I can to sense that other thinking. Now I remember that I had that in my philosophy studies, but I didn't recognize it. Of course, there was nobody like Johannes around who could point that out to me … That what I am now sensing in thinking, is a different way of thinking than the 'thinking' that the computer can do. I don't want to say that I already have it, but I do have something in my memory that I can hold on to."

Els shook her head in bewilderment and she said:

"You're so incredibly gifted … If it turns out that that giftedness also works in that other way of thinking … "

"I don't mean to say that … For the time being I haven't got that, but I'm going to use all the power of my giftedness to try to understand what this other thinking is. And when you understand it, you'll probably find it."

After dinner, after they had tidied up everything, they both wanted to try to think about 1 once more. They had refrained from the usual drink before dinner and the glass of wine, from an intuitive suspicion that that would make such a thought exercise difficult. So they both retreated into themselves.

Initially Raymond had great difficulty concentrating. Ordinary intellectual thinking always pulled him away from the number 1. Everything he had found on the internet in half an hour wanted to crawl into his mind and prevented him from looking at the 1 as a concept, in a concentrated way. Until he realized that he could, of course, also consciously think about the facts he had found: around the 1, as it were, making that single point concept richer and more filled.

When he started with that, he felt a strange familiar thing, of which he wasn't actually sure whether he had ever experienced it as consciously, except perhaps during that time when he had occupied himself with Plato. It was as if the familiar number 1, with which he had learned to calculate, became a shadow area. Not in the present and not immediately here, a light seemed to shine, that the insight into and the awareness of the 1 was a concept. It was as if a memory came to mind of something, which a human being apparently knows, but which he alone is not aware of. When that comes to consciousness, it does not lie in the here and now, but lives as a memory of something that once was.

He was touched even more by that, than by the understanding of unity. He shifted into a completely different mood. He also remembered that mood. In the form of light it could come to him when he played the piano. Now the mood got so strong that he thought he would be overwhelmed by it. An overwhelming memory lay behind that number 1.

He sighed, opened his eyes, got back into his normal routine where all this was unknown and tried again.

He now really tried to turn his attention to the meaning of the number 1.

Again, an overwhelming memory of unity came to him, an existence in which there was no sense of separateness or division whatsoever and which was not empty, either. Its existence was filled with everything that could be, but was not yet ...

Of course, he had read such reports on the internet. They hadn't told him much, except that it was interesting. Now, the concept brought with it the overwhelming effect of his remembering…

The emotion became so intense that he began to weep. Els, frightened, stopped her exercise and said:

"Raymond, what's wrong?!!!"

"I don't have words for this … " he said, sobbing. "I really don't know what's happening! But that this is an aspect of thinking that a computer could never, ever have, that penetrates me painfully."

The tears ran down his cheeks for so long, until the shameful embarrassment about his own vision for the future had ebbed away.

The next morning everything seemed like a bad dream and he united himself again with his familiar thoughts, of which he had been so deeply mortified yesterday …

At ten o'clock Johannes was waiting for them in the hall and he said:

"Before we talk, let's go to the master. I have arranged it with him, and it is better to visit him than to have him visit us."

"Exciting … " said Raymond.

They walked out of the building, down the path to a chalet set slightly lower down, which they saw in the distance.

Johannes said:

"Decades ago he saved me, as it were, from my rigid intellect. I could not follow him in everything, so I did not become his apprentice permanently. But we have been able to exchange and fertilize our ways, and we still do. He will tell you in detail where he comes from, where he is now and where he is going - and what he sees as his task as part of the work we do here."

Small but impressive, he opened the door himself. He offered Raymond and Els his hand and touched Johannes on the upper arm. He spoke Dutch reasonably well and so the conversation could be conducted in Dutch.

They sat down in a study. The atmosphere was half oriental, half monastic. The room was filled with a benevolent atmosphere and it was not clear where that atmosphere came from, except from the presence of the master himself. You would say the work he did in this room must have radiated this benevolent atmosphere …

They sat down, it remained hushed for a moment. The master observed the two visitors, not intrusively, but full of interest. Then he began to speak.

" Johannes has already told me a few things. I come from the Far East, I was raised and ordained in a Buddhist monastery, and when I had received my ordination, and had spent a number of years in that monastery as an ordained monk, the great master who was invisibly present there and to whom you were admitted only in exceptional cases, more or less sent me as a missionary to Europe. I lived in complete surrender to the master's will. It would not have occurred to me to oppose this intention of his. But it pained me to have to leave my beloved homeland, the beautiful surroundings of the monastery, and to go to an area where it was clear to us that the people there, although intelligent, were loveless …

"That is how I came here, and I worked for many years in this institute, which was made available to me, to teach the people who came here out of an interest in Eastern spirituality, something of love. That love which, in our opinion, should also flow through all knowledge. And so I was lonely here. Occasionally there was someone with whom I could feel some form of relationship. Until a time when a young girl came here several consecutive years in the summer. That's Eva. In her I really got to know a loving European, a soul so overflowing with love, that you could feel: this human being can move mountains out of love!

"That encounter was surpassed. Johannes came to sit at my bedside at one point, when I was in the Netherlands, because I had been admitted with an almost fatal pneumonia. We talked to each other and I was stunned by his light. Not white light, but coloured light, like that reflected in a diamond.

But even with him, I missed that love. His love was for his discipline, for his profession. But I felt that he had disengaged himself from sensory reality as it is in nature. I wanted to restore that to him. I had the feeling: here you are facing the light, which rises in the west - that's Johannes. But he wasn't finding happiness …

"He came here then as well - but couldn't be my disciple.

"I will spare you the difficult times we went through - until we found each other again and I gradually understood that my judgment of this had been completely wrong. I had judged something that I could not see, it escaped my powers of observation: because I couldn't see it, I thought it wasn't there …

"Once I realized who I was dealing with in this Johannes, I gave him my entire work and the entire institute.

"So, now we have been here together for decades and I hope will still have time to see how the world develops, to incorporate my strength for a positive outcome.

"My task, as I see it, nurtured by my innate capacities and by the initiation I have undergone, is to make all this available to the impoverished Westerner who has been stripped of inner wisdom, again and again. I have the ability to immerse myself completely in nature and to be continually aware both of myself and the divine in it. Before I knew Johannes, I lost myself in the perception of nature. Thanks to the exercises I was enabled to do with Johannes, I no longer lose my self-awareness while still having the ability to be completely immersed in nature. I grow and blossom with nature, but I also get closer to the earth element, I flow with the water element, I blow with the air and I burn with the fire … . I know the nature of lightning and thunder, of the gathering of the clouds. I know the essential quality of the different animals when I perceive them, and I am so engrossed in them that I feel this animal nature from within.

"That's what I'm trying to show people here, to show them how you do that. I know that in the antiquity of European culture it was Persephone, the goddess Natura, who, together with the human soul, gave the soul the ability I have…"

He looked at Raymond and said:

"That's how I can blend in with your nature, too, Raymond. I know that you scientists have the most complicated test procedures to get to the bottom of what the brain actually does. From my point of view, as I really see it, behold it, that's a pretty ridiculous idea. If I may sketch it in an image: there is no organ that is as complacent and lazy - you may also say: living in surrender – as the brain. It really never does anything! Just as the moon does not radiate any light from itself, so there is no activity whatsoever in the brain. And what you think you perceive as activity, that is surrender, that is recording and reproduction, that is reflection as in a mirror. A mirror does nothing itself, the one who is doing the reflecting is the one doing something.

126

"I see the brain lying lazily in a comfortable chair, observing everything, doing nothing. And when I look at you, Raymond, I see an unhealthy domination of that passivity of the brain. You're so intelligent because you're so adept at reflecting, mirroring everything around you. But you wouldn't discover the reality of that until your other pole, your opposite pole, your 'will' pole became active.

"If you stay the way you are now, you can't really stay healthy - excuse me for saying so! But you won't stay the way you are, because you've met Johannes! And when he starts caring about you … I don't think many people will stay the way they are … He keeps calling on you to change yourself, and he does it so you have to hear it. Believe me, I speak from experience …

"I've heard that you see a future ahead of you, in which the annual exponential growth of computational capacity of artificial intelligence will unite itself with the computational capacity of the human brain, which will then gradually turn out to appear ridiculously clumsy and small. Cosmic wisdom has to be taken over by machines that calculate their decisions: yes or no."

He saw that Raymond wanted to protest and raised his hand. He went on:

"I know there are other systems - but you can be assured, it isn't true. The machine has been given the right name: computer. You're imagining, and you're thinking that all it takes is from all those possibilities to calculate solutions, and you don't realize that by doing so you are excluding what *life* is, and putting some kind of 'anti-life' in its place. You might as well forget that 'anti-life', the cosmos really doesn't need that! But if this continues, then I can guarantee you that in the cosmos there will be a large cancerous tumour caused by these artificial brain functions, which will disrupt the whole life of the planet, and the cosmos. Don't believe that this will lead to any positive results. That is my vision for the future, and I perceive what is happening in the world in the field of science with fear and trembling. We in the East have an eye for that; also, the most talent. You will know that the trade with this strange virtual currency, the bitcoin, is mainly occurring in China. When you delve into what this whole new coin system is all about, you get the impression that you are being magnificently tricked; even though you can't exactly put your finger on the precise location of this deception. But it is clear that it is a mockery. All such things that become possible with modern technology are handy – but are, in fact, superfluous.

"I don't need a nanobot to penetrate my brain and explore what's happening there. As you know, nothing is being done there, but the system of surrender might eventually be discovered. I don't need that! We have in our initiation tradition the effective meaning of the mantram: AUM!!!

"For thousands of years, the technique has been known how to use your inner investigative powers to probe the windings of your brain to find out who you are and what you can know. All this you can then give back to the divinity in surrender and gratitude. But I have found it in this place, it can also be found in modern spiritual science. Once you know that fact, then perhaps you can understand that modern science must be judged as blind, incapable of any concrete examination of any organ in the human body.

"There is a method of descending with one's own consciousness into the depths of the body. You will hear about that over the next few days. And I hope - and also wish this for you - that when you leave here you will realize that you have been wasting your strength for about thirty years, and that you will realize that it is never too late to use your strength where it should be used.

"You're highly gifted, yes, Raymond. But I'm telling you, it's a sin that that giftedness has become addicted to the tree of knowledge!"

Raymond felt he had been listening to a thundering storm. Without a principle of true or false, he could not make a judgement about it at this moment in time. When a violent thunderstorm breaks loose and it thunders, you don't ask whether the thunder is speaking the truth. But you know: the thunderstorm *itself* is true! And so it was, with this thundering speech, too.

Raymond was not used to criticism and certainly not being punished for omitting something. Maybe he had also carefully avoided that by always doing his best and doing things the way they were expected of him. Now he was being reprimanded because he had always done what was expected of him!

According to this 'god of thunder', what had been expected of him had apparently been the wrong thing. If he had been a child he would have started to cry now - and had he been alone, he would have done the same. But now, in the company of three adults, each the best in his field, of course he could not. It was as if his mind had been removed from his head and as if he only had a heart. That heart was deeply embarrassed, just as he had been the previous night. But he couldn't work out whether it was right that he should be so mortified, because for that he needed his mind …

The master smiled and said:

"It's not easy, such an unusual conversation. Moreover, it's been a monologue on my part - you haven't had a chance to say anything yourself.

"But that's why I'm the master!

"Think again about whether what I said could be true.

"If you come to the conclusion that what I said is true, don't be upset and don't sin again!!"

The master arose to signal the end of the conversation. He took them to the door and when he shook Raymond's hand he said:

"You're angry, aren't you, Raymond? You shouldn't be! You can't be angry with the truth, can you? The point is that I want to call on you earnestly to take a critical look at what modern science has taught you. You rely on what is supposedly proven, but I would say: study the theory of knowledge you use, you are a philosopher too, aren't you? You young people in this Western world - but also in the east, in a different way - are slaves of science. You have no faith, you say, but your faith lies with that holy house of science! No one is allowed to touch that! I want to make you aware of that. I think it's a great shame what you are doing, I think it's a great shame that you are doing it, too! That's my vision - and again, if you have another one, then forget what I've told you!"

Raymond was pale and nodded silently.

"Thank you for your honesty … " After all, he was angry.

The master said goodbye to Els and Johannes and they walked back along the path to the main building. Els asked Johannes:

"Why is he so stern?!?"

Johannes said:

"He says what he thinks. He is truthful through and through, not careful or cautious, that's true … He's hurt a lot of people and has turned them against him. I know all about it, he treated me the same way when I first came here. I was not allowed to join the esoteric lessons because the presence of my mind would disturb it! I wasn't happy about that, either. But I can tell you, I have known him for decades now and he is thoroughly sincere. He looks right through you and if he thinks it does you good when he tells you what he sees, then he pronounces it. Come, Raymond!" he said, "you need a cup of coffee! Let's sit down on the terrace together, it's nice now and we can have a chat there."

"I wanted to tell you about my experiences with the number 1 yesterday … "

" Let's see how far we get … " said Johannes and preceded them to a table by the terrace doors. The whole terrace was empty.

Johannes was still a real 'chef' in this company. You felt the respect of passers-by and Els and Raymond were included. They sat down and Johannes ordered coffee. Raymond got a bit of colour back and said:

"I am indeed very angry with that man. Why does he have to attack me like that, when I have built up my scientific vision from a certain innocence?"

Johannes said:

"The last thing he said to you in the doorway, that's what he sees as your guilt, that with your great mind you're not critical of the scientific method you're working with. If you were, you wouldn't have so easily assumed the research results to be true. We have already talked about it, there are a lot of assumptions that are interconnected, and then supported by some research results, as truth. This is what the master objects to and, of course, I agree with him because I know about the – using an old-fashioned word - blasphemous language used by the proponents of singularity and trans- and post-humanism. I looked it up again in that fat book by Kurzweil. When you read that book, you often have the impression that you're in a science fiction film. But he substantiates his science fiction with concrete research results and of course it is admirable how much he is aware of the progress of that research. Although this book is already very old - because what is fourteen years? An eternity, when technical development goes as fast as he would have us believe. He has made a number of predictions that have come true, but you can also see in this book a whole series of predictions for our time that you really can't say have come true by now."

"Exactly!" Els said, "I'm always saying that, too! It's better to look at what does *not* come true than what *does*. Then you have to get over the fact that you find everything so impressive."

Johannes nodded, took his phone out of his pocket, found what he was looking for, and read out some quotes:

" 'Eventually, our intelligence will penetrate the entire universe. This is the purpose of the universe. Instead of the 'stupid', simple, mechanical forces of celestial mechanics, we will then decide on our own survival.'

" 'Something more controversial than brain research is uploading a brain. Brain uploading means scanning a brain down to the smallest detail and reproducing it in another suitable medium. This would capture a person's personality and all of their memories and abilities.' "

"I saved these to remind you once again that when you make such statements, you really need to know very well what you're talking about."

Raymond said:

"I'm familiar with those statements, of course. I know them by heart, so to speak, and I was passionate about them, until about ten days ago…. Now I'm very different, already, and that's not pleasant, I can tell you. It's like throwing away all the certainties of your scientific knowledge and then the question arises: What are you? What do you have to use your intelligence for, then? Isn't all this just a dream that, when I'm at home, turns out to be a nightmare? But then I won't be able to find my old self again. I feel cut in two: one half tends towards you, even towards that strict master, who is sincere, of course - I've actually seen that. And maybe shaking everything up, also works … But the other side is accustomed to the thought patterns you have just read out, and of course it's not just Kurzweil. Philosophically, the Jesuit Teilhard de Chardin is an important pillar for this vision of the future. That man really had a connection with Christianity. I have been thinking about myself - that I don't believe in anything except what has been proven. Now the master is shaking up that foundation under me by saying: 'You have a different faith, namely the faith in science, the results of which are very dubious. So, you're a believer as well and you think for sure it's true, but you haven't looked at the reliability of the process of knowing, at all!' Of course, we believe that we are trying to find out the reliability of the knowledge process with the help of reverse engineering of the brain, which is impressive. When you know that in Europe, for example, as I said, a big project is going on concerning the human brain, in which hundreds of leading scientists are participating, with tens of millions in grants from the EU every year! Am I supposed to think it's all nonsense? That all these great scholars have not considered whether their theory of knowledge is reliable?"

"Well … " said Johannes. "But if you, as a leading thinker, aren't thinking more deeply about the reliability of scientific research, why should those others?"

"Do you actually know what you're saying, Johannes?"

Johannes's steel blue eyes looked straight into Raymond's eyes.

"Yes, of course," Raymond said with a sigh. "Of course, you know what you're saying. But maybe you understand, I'm shocked! I'd rather run away, turn the clock back to before this damned holiday, when I was still a foolish believer in science. Now I feel I have no choice but to go into opposition - opposition to conventional natural science - and I don't want that! It's nice to belong to that ordinary science college. And look what Teilhard de Chardin had to say about all this!"

He then picked up his own phone, looked up the text and quoted:

" 'Isn't it impressive how these many devices are, as it were, created and developed in solidarity? More and more, all the machines of the Earth as a whole are striving to form one big, organized machine. The technical branches in turn bend into each other, accelerating and multiplying their progress until they form one gigantic complex that encompasses the entire planet. Who is the carrier, the inventive core of this immeasurable device, if not the mental world?'

And:

" 'How is the connection of the Earth's reflective elements to be made? Of course, via the news networks and the calculators, which connect us all in a kind of 'etheric' consciousness. So they anticipate a direct coordination of the brain with each other by means of the still mysterious forces of telepathy.'

"Johannes, I….I feel like I have lost my mind. There, where my comprehension was, there is a void. I can still carry on talking and I know what I am saying, too - I have not suddenly become demented - but the whole content of my mind suddenly seems to be worthless."

"Of course, that's not true," said Johannes. "The value of that content is that you know through and through what is being developed in technology, and how certain currents of hard artificial intelligence want to lead those scientific results to some sort of cosmic machine. Whether that is a real possibility I cannot foresee. But that they actually see that as a real possibility, that is clear. From the spiritual insights we have, we are really taking this very seriously. For we know that there is a tendency, that is growing ever stronger, that is based on a certain spiritual power that indeed wants to replace the spiritual intelligence in the cosmos with machine intelligence. That had already been anticipated before this development really started. So, here, we are taking this really seriously and, in that sense, it is very valuable that you are aware of all those investigations and research methods. I don't mind that you went along with them for a while. The master sees it as a kind of mortal sin and from his perspective I can understand that, too. But from the perspective of having had more experience with science, I see it in a rather more nuanced way. You really don't have to erase all science and clear your mind now, please don't do that! That can remain in full bloom; only - and the master is right about this - you should test your faith in it, critique it, look for the points where science is absolutely truthful, and where it ends up in quicksand."

Raymond said:

"I don't feel like I've been given any tools to do that during my development - testing my faith in science, critiquing the scientific method. I'm used to going with the flow and it's precisely because I don't resist, that absorbing knowledge is so easy. When I have to start thinking about the knowledge I absorb: how was it obtained, is it reliable, where are the possibilities of error? I can take note of it, but I don't have to believe it? - then it's going to be very difficult to make any headway. So I have become quite distraught by this visit to the master! Last night, after Els and I, each on our own, had done an examination of the being, the understanding of the number 1, I was in a similar state. I think I've had a good look at that other thinking you're talking about. And so it has also become a reality, not fiction, but truly an existing reality, which I actually know and remember very well. There were times in

133

my college days when I was within it, but there's no one to tell you that you're in it, so you leave it, and don't value it. Now, last night I was deeply embarrassed about myself, for denying that other way of thinking: and I already sensed a guilty feeling within myself, which I have laid on myself, by assuming as true these kinds of thinking which you have just read to me. Without testing them. I always told myself, as a kind of excuse, that the priest and Jesuit Teilhard de Chardin sees a moral dimension to the whole. In this way the two visions corresponded and I always thought that it would be a good thing if this technical development proceeded the way it is projected to go. I also don't feel too easy about the idea that they are all illusions, because in research practice a lot does become real, albeit indirectly, but still…. So, what is presented in this so-called science fiction seemed to me to be a matter of time only, and all these things will happen, I thought, because they are well grounded scientifically.

"I am now confused. I am now thinking: maybe we shouldn't want that at all, that that's going to happen and then there are two possibilities: either it has been fiction, and then it won't happen anyway; or it has a basis of reality, and then a battle would have to be commenced to prevent these prospects from eventually becoming a reality. Even if only ten percent of it were true, that would still be too much. And ten percent seems to me to be true, anyway. The computer does have the potential to calculate solutions for problems that human beings cannot find. I do feel now that those solutions can point in the wrong direction. But that doesn't mean that they can't also lead to reality. And if you're saying that you know from spiritual investigation that there is a power that is striving for this change in the cosmos, then that could very well come about."

"That is why it is very important that you do not lose your mental capacities, that you do not lose the content of your scientific thinking, that you continue to pursue what is being discovered in science. But - as far as we are concerned - without actually believing in all of that."

"If you say yourself," Raymond said, "that it is not entirely untrue, this vision of the future, that it is indeed intended by a certain power, why then should I not believe in it?"

"You will have to have more knowledge of the different processes involved in the development of mankind, so that you will learn to understand what is healthy and what is not. I believe that's what it's all about: health, in the broadest sense of the word."

"This is getting worse and worse … "

"What do you mean?"

"That I've lost my mind. I've always had the impression that I do understand how things are and where I stand. Now I'm totally losing it, there's nothing left of it. Even if I continue to take care of the whole content of my scientific knowledge, as you explain to me, I still have the feeling that I am losing my mental capacity."

Johannes nodded slowly and said:

"You're out of balance, that's understandable. You'll find it again, don't worry."

Raymond said:

"Are you staying alert to the principle of freedom, here?"

"You mean - you've been handled so hard?"

" Yes."

"There was freedom in that interlude of the master's forceful statement, whether you can perceive what he said or not. If you decide to close your mind to that, or if you were to say, 'I don't agree' - then everything he said lapses".

"Yes, yes … " said Raymond. "I think I understand that … "

They didn't feel like going for a long walk and strolled down the path in the park. There was a way down and they wanted to go down it a bit and then back to the car. After a couple of hundred meters there was a sign: 'DANGER: ROAD CLOSED!'

They stopped. Raymond looked into the distance and said:

"I think that's an exaggeration. Let's just get past this … "

"No way!" said Els. "I'm not going to do that; you know, that sign is there for a reason!"

"Come on, we don't want to go that far. We'll just walk up to where the road is closed … "

"It says it's dangerous!"

Raymond shrugged his shoulders and walked off along the path, but Els stayed put. He assumed she'd follow him, but she didn't … When he looked back he saw her waiting in the distance. He thought to himself, "How stubborn you are!" but then he turned to go back to her. As he came closer, he felt his great love for this sensible, beautiful woman. He ran up to her, lifted her up, twirled her around and said:

"If I didn't have you, we'd be lying dead down there somewhere."

"Well, you must be tired of life," she said. "Let's just go home … "

They walked a bit further through the park and saw the small clinic. They retraced their steps and went back to the car park.

Raymond had turned in on himself and Els wondered how to extricate him from it, from this deep sense of being insulted.

She said:

"Come on, Raymond, we can take a beating, can't we?"

"I don't understand why anyone should insult me like that! He could have spoken with a little more sensitivity, couldn't he?"

"That wouldn't have worked - I've tried that myself so many times! I have to tell you, I'm thankful he said it straight from the heart."

"Bah … " said Raymond and he sat down. "And yet you're right about something. I'm deeply offended, I really am. But on the other hand, it's also done me some good. As if you were suddenly pushed into the deep water and had a bracing swim. You take a very deep breath, you come out again and you feel like you've been reborn. The feeling is not pleasant, but the effect is."

"That man is a Wise One, he really knows what he's saying and doing. And I don't believe he does anything without love. He did it out of love."

"What are you saying … I have the feeling that we've ended up on Olympus, where, as you know, one has no business to be! Apollo, and Zeus, the god of thunder, we've already met. I wonder what the next meeting will bring us … These days are passing with an intensity that a human being wouldn't normally experience in a whole year."

"If that's Olympus," Els smiled, "we are even living above it now! But if you say it like that, then this is the singularity - when there is an exponentially increasing intensity of experience and you are dealing with something that is of a cosmic order!"

"What are you saying!"

"I mean, by singularity you mean that all the usual known laws lose their meaning and that something sort of explodes, causing the whole of existence - space and time and the people - to take on a different

136

form. That is what you call 'singularity' and you envisage it as a capacity of artificial intelligence, through which the computational capacity of Man increases to such an extent, thanks to AI, that what you can then do in a second, you cannot do now in a whole lifetime. Isn't that what it is?"

"It's something like that … " Raymond said with a sigh.

"Now, you are saying yourself that the intensity of experience here is so much greater, and unprecedented, than in life in the city and your ordinary existence. That's a kind of singularity: not in being able to calculate and store data and reproduce it again and find solutions, but in the form of an enormous increase in the intensity of life in every second!"

"Yes, you're right about that … " he said. "This is indeed unprecedented. What one experiences here in a day, or in fact only in an hour or two, changes one's life in such a way that I know for sure, that when we go down again - and I really mean back to the city, back home - the old laws will no longer be applicable. I'm curious what's in store for us; and whether those other characters here are of such a calibre, and have as much to say to me … "

"And to me, too … " Els added.

The next morning at 10 o'clock they were back in Johannes' room. He asked:

"And? Have you sensed anything of the other thinking I've been talking about?"

Raymond said:

"Yes, I mentioned yesterday that I sensed a form of thinking in a flash, that I recognise from my studies and maybe from even before that. Where it's not about factual knowledge, but where something else, which lies behind it, lights up like a flash and warms and illuminates your whole being. For a moment I understood that the 1 is more than a number with which you can calculate. For a moment I also understood - and I remember this, but I don't have the concept now, I have to extract it from my memory - that for a moment I knew what undividedness is, unity in the original sense of the word. At that moment I was very touched by this and also felt briefly that I should indeed be mortified at the loss of this thinking capacity in favour of my calculating capacity. I looked at the 2 in the half hour that we allow ourselves to view the internet, because that will undoubtedly be today's theme?"

Johannes nodded.

"Then, to my amazement, I see that there is a whole spiritual science about the 2, that it goes back to Pythagoras, probably to other great spiritual teachers before that, and that Plato was the one who passed it on. It is said that he did not write down what he knew, but that he passed it on by word of mouth. That would be Plato's unwritten writings. In them, the 2 as Dyade come to full appearance. This has been reconstructed from certain pieces of Aristotle's text, which seems to refer to it, and also from later texts, which also show that such writings of Plato, which were passed on orally, did exist." Johannes smiled and said:

"You acquire a lot of knowledge in half an hour!"

"Yes, factual knowledge indeed … " said Raymond. "But naturally I did think about it for a while afterwards and, although I did not come to the experience of that other thinking, I found it very interesting to see for oneself how the indivisibility splits into two, creating the *contradiction*.

"Aristotle calls these contradictions by name and refers to Plato and Pythagoras. They are the primal opposites in existence. When you think about them, you feel a bit of it. You feel that we humans are also caught up in these opposites and that the moment we feel happy we are in balance between those two opposites for a moment. But at that point, actually, the 2 is already 'conquered', I suppose."

Johannes shook his head and said:

"You're quite capable!"

Els said:

"Yes Johannes, as you'll find out! It's really incredible what he's doing, they've seen it at school and university! But no one perceives it as well as I do, because I live with him. It's a miracle how he collects his knowledge, remembers it and links it all together."

"It becomes clear to me at the same time," Raymond said, "that this way of dealing with numbers is really something quite different from what arithmetic has become in our time. With us, numbers are abstract; you can see that also with scientists. They like to talk about millions and billions, which is so easy to do in a written document. But of course it is not the case, that when such a thing is said or written, the speaker or writer also has in mind how big that number actually is. A billion units - just saying that shows that the unit is not a unit. You connect a number to it and that has already become something very abstract, I have sensed that. In the end, this understanding of number looks more like a collection of linguistic or logical concepts, because a meaning is attached to the number."

"Excuse me," said Johannes, "because the number has a meaning?"

"You can't turn 1 into something other than what it is, that's what arithmetic is. But the whole world of understanding that appears to be connected to it has a similarity with other concepts. The moral concept, for example. When you talk about love, you can also do so abstractly, so that you use the word without having a well-defined idea for yourself of what love actually is. This is the way we deal with numbers all the time - and when I say it like this, I realize again how bad it really is.

"But on the other hand, of course, you wouldn't make any progress in arithmetic if you had to be aware of that all the time."

"You don't have to be aware of that all the time! If you regularly withdraw into yourself and look for the world of concepts that belongs to a number, that is enough to hold onto reality; and, while abstracting, use that way of thinking when you start calculating again, and forget the concepts. That does not have to bother you any further then; but as, let's say, a 'call to attention' that that world is present in your thinking capacity, then you will not easily make the kinds of statements which I read to you yesterday, and which are common in the world of hard artificial intelligence anyway. You simply won't get that past your lips anymore, because you know that the whole conceptual world of number is, as it were, squeezed out of that computational capacity. If you had solely the computational capacity left over and cultivated that, then you would have cultivated the husk - which you usually throw away in everyday life, while you enjoy the juice."

"So - you are actually saying that if I studied the meaning of the numbers in that other way of thinking on a daily basis, I wouldn't 'sin so easily', as the master puts it?"

"It will turn out that other things are needed, but this is a very fruitful start. Of course, it's about not just assuming on logical grounds that this thinking of which I speak - "

Raymond interrupted him and said:

"That's not going to happen anytime soon - because I don't think it's that logical!"

"That you don't accept it for that reason ... " Johannes went on, "but that you accept it because you feel that it exists."

"That's already happened ... " Raymond said. "That's why I'm feeling - and I still do - that I have lost my mental compass ... "

"That is because your mind is used to arithmetic and has learned to ignore the whole world of concepts, not only of arithmetic, but also of the other concepts that are the instruments in our thinking. That is why you think that your capacity to calculate is the actual mind. When that threatens to lose its value, you think you may also lose your mind. But you were also a child once, and a child does not yet work with calculating capacity, but lives very simply in that other world of concepts."

Els said:

"That's when he got kicked out, after only three years. Of course, they all loved it, how smart that little boy was and fed it - overfed it."

"That's a pity … " said Johannes. "With me, in my youth, it didn't work out. I was, so to speak, the stupidest little boy in the classroom and if my father hadn't had such a clear realisation that I wanted to stay in that different way of thinking, my computational capacity would have remained completely asleep! But it would have been awakened anyway, even though I was in high school at the time. That makes it much easier for me, because in my memory I have a conscious recollection of that world, of that other thinking."

"And yet," said Raymond, "I haven't completely lost that world either, I think that's thanks to my interest in astronomy. I read and I read and I read! I went to the library, I wanted to read this book and that book, and I read books that were far too difficult for my age. But I also read old books, especially later. When I was in high school I read Johannes Kepler's book about the Harmony of the World. Well, you can sense that different thinking …   and I still carry that with me. It appears as soon as I sit down and start thinking about the 1 and the 2. Once I get going with that, then that world lights up and when I am within it, then I know: these have been the most valuable moments in my life, when I have caught a glimpse of it. I have been confusing that, with the joy of arithmetic. Of course, that's nice too, if you can do it well - and you always get the correct answers and you are praised, and so on and so forth. Yet that is joy from the outside; but those fruits from the inside - I really remember them. I had told you about Ficino or Plato, but this astronomy from the start of the Enlightenment has brought me such moments, too. In those days, fragments of that other way of thinking probably still had the upper hand."

"Do you see, Johannes?" Els said. "I've always seen this in him. I've always thought: no one sees that, they only see his unbelievably quick grasp and his gigantic memory. But that' s not really him. If what he really is could emerge - I think we'd be surprised!'

Raymond said:
"I do wonder if you are serious enough about the extent of this singularity movement. Here you are with a handful of people on a mountain, and I'm sure you have your network in Europe, but it's probably not

very pervasive and extensive. In contrast, there is the network of singularity that appeals to many younger intellectuals who also enjoy communicating and brainstorming with each other on the internet, setting up research projects, sharing that with their partners and friends in the community, their fellows - and forming a strong global community of people who not only believe in this futuristic idea but who are also determined to make it happen."

"Maybe you're right," Johannes said, "that I'm not taking it seriously enough. However, I am taking it sufficiently seriously to set aside an hour or two every day for a fortnight for you, but of course that's only a small amount. I thought I was taking it seriously, but maybe there's a bit of disbelief around in the ability to disseminate this worldview widely, because most people take no account at all of that other thinking and the communities that are working with that other thinking - and they're often not that visible."

"What do you mean?!?' Raymond asked.

"What I mean is that there are creative and up-building spiritual powers that are much, much stronger, more powerful and more intelligent than you or anything you can ever imagine, but which leave mankind free to discover for itself that the world of appearances - with all its technology - is actually an unnecessary extra, and certainly not a possible replacement. But perhaps I should reconsider my unbelief, for it is of course true that I recognise the power behind it: an invisible power, too, but one that has an extraordinarily powerful intelligence which it works to enrich with creative human intelligence that it does not itself have. The danger is great, maybe even greater than I think is possible.

"But I know Him just as well, even better, that other Lord, who is the true source of all intelligence, and whose technical intelligence has been stolen, more or less. That other Lord embraces that original thinking, and I simply cannot imagine that at some point there will not be some intervention that will prevent this development from taking place."

"What," said Raymond, "if this intervention were expected *from you*?"

Johannes became silent and took his head in his hands. A deep silence fell …

Then Johannes murmured:
"As I said, I need to think about this in depth."

"Look," said Raymond, "the point is that this group of technicians and scientists are all very intellectually gifted and that they look down on all those people, who are so fond of their biological brains and their other nature, with a kind of contempt. Someone has even suggested that human speech - for these highly developed KI people – will be something akin to what the mooing of cows is for us now."

"For God's sake!" exclaimed Els.

"Yes, that shows how they actually despise biological nature and elevate that wonderful technical intellect, that I love so much myself, to the highest accolades – far above all natural evolution. I have no reason to doubt its realizability. Whether it appears as fast as some predict is something else - that is not to be hoped for - but that such a thing could be possible, I certainly do not think that is out of the question. As you know, I have committed myself to this as well. I know what it feels like when you engage with such a future perspective, and I also know all the misleading arguments in favour of it.

"What do you think will happen to me when I leave this road and go your way? A chorus of despicable ridicule will be heaped upon me!"

Johannes said:

"You don't have to reveal what you've learned here straight away. I would very much appreciate it if you would fulfil your function as a professor in Amsterdam for a number of years."

"Of course," said Raymond, "I'm not ready for such decisions. I just want to say that these people have a certain approach and that you'd rather stay out of it when you turn away from that. Even though it all looks very informal and cheerful. For me the most important thing now is: how can I find more stability in that other thinking? I have assured myself completely that it exists. But I'm used to living in that one mode of thinking. Should I look up literature that stimulates that other thinking? For example, should I study that big fat book by Johannes Kepler again and see if it evokes that other thinking in me? I could go back to Ficino's books again, too, and try to remember what that was like in my student days. Would you think that's the right thing to do?"

"Partly," Johannes said. "On the other hand, it will be important that you do your daily practice of the other thinking. In your case, I think the best way to do that is by understanding number. We've touched the 2 today; we can come back to that tomorrow and then move on to the 3. I promised Eva that we would visit her. She's probably already waiting for us, let's go!"

They now walked the other way, along the path where they had taken a short walk the day before, to the clinic. It turned out to be a beautiful, tasteful, modern building with lots of light, soft colours, many natural materials.

"You'd wouldn't mind being sick here!" Els said. "What a delight!"

Johannes led them down the corridor to Eva's room. She was already there.

They sat, as usual in this community, in the armchairs, not around the desk.

"Shall I just start?" said Eva.

Johannes nodded and she began to speak:

"It was here that I met Johannes, as you know, when he came here for the first time. As for me, I was seeking food for my longing soul. Longing for depth, for authenticity, for love. I had not received that much of it at home. My father was tough and my mother a bit distant. There was no significant religious life, although we did go to church.

"At the master's I found part of what I was looking for. He, too, was strict - like my father. I remember not being allowed to talk for a few days once, I don't remember why. He took measures like that. And, oh dear if you didn't stick to it!

"But I soon got closer to him when it turned out we both had great affection for Johannes. And so a bond for life was formed. When Johannes and I had children, he came to look after our children in the winter! Can you imagine that? I went to the Conservatoire and did my piano studies while I was already a doctor. It was only here that I really became a medical practitioner. I studied a lot with Johannes in spiritual medical literature, starting with Hippocrates and, I think, ending with Rudolf Steiner. Throughout the entire history of human development, in which Man is concerned about his physical body, I have learned to experience and acknowledge that the human body is a sanctuary, that the cosmos has become a physical body which, for a period of time on earth, is a residence for you. You have the cosmos outside of you, but in a certain sense you have also become one, in so far as you are or have a body. The powers to do so do not come from the DNA, but from the Cosmos."

"But the DNA is a fact!" Raymond objected.

"Of course! It certainly belongs to the blueprint of heredity. But that's not the actual human being, and that's not the actual form of the physical body, either. In the same way that there is another way of thinking in addition to the computational capacity, there is another way of thinking about the DNA body. That body indeed also has to do with health and disease. If you can look at it that way, then you see the spirit of Man has metamorphosed into a physical body – a temple.

"In preparation for this conversation I watched a number of videos on YouTube by Robert Freitas and also read some fragments on the internet, how he and his people imagine that they can make nano-computers, no bigger than red blood cells, which can be injected and then directed via a computer. In such a way, that where they can do research from the inside, they can do that; and where they can be therapeutically effective, they can also do that. The temple of the physical body is then populated with countless machines, devices. I sometimes wonder how it is possible for people who work with the physical body to think that such a thing is possible?"

"It's already being tested in animal experiments!" Raymond said.

"Of course, it might be possible to do this as well. I don't mean that," she said. "I mean, that you can justify - morally and with your emotions and, of course, ultimately with your mind - sending an army of microrobots into a temple."

"But that army has the best of intentions for the temple!" Raymond exclaimed.

"But…. it has the capacity to completely desecrate that temple. You probably don't know that everything that comes into the human being from the outside world - whether it's sensory impressions or nutrients or air or whatever - is made human before it can be used. Anything you absorb that you do not make your own, turns against you.

"Thanks to Johannes's insights, I have also learned that this is true with thoughts, as well. When you constantly think thoughts that you have not tested in such a way that you have made them your own, then you include a foreign element within your whole mind. As a result, it becomes more and more complicated and difficult for that other world to work with that other thinking and those other hierarchies within you. You alienate yourself from that and you are less and less able to stand up against that foreign thinking. If you start to think that through, then this ongoing development is a colossal disaster. The moment a possibility arises to bring technically developed particles into the human body, something will arise that is certainly unprecedented.

"In spiritual cosmology we know of the earth's development in several successive phases and each phase has an ascent, a climax and then a descent. If you look at the phase that precedes ours, it was a culture in which at some point people had developed the ability to experiment with life itself. That spelt the end of that culture. In the Bible, we know that end by the name of the Flood … "

"That didn't really happen," said Raymond, falling back into his familiar patterns of thought.

"You can say that," she said, "but have you really tested what you're saying now? Isn't that just an assumption you're making now, based on everything you've read in scientific research?

"Be that as it may, I have devoted my entire life to learning and maintaining the health of that human temple, and I believe I am achieving something with it. There are three of us - Philippe's wife, whom you will meet, my colleague here and then there is Peter, whom you will also meet, who is in charge of what we call 'the outpatient clinic'. That's actually a kind of doctor's surgery, for first aid in case of accidents. He's pretty busy there in the high season. As far as our knowledge base is concerned, we are supported by Johannes, Philippe, Beato, whom you will also meet. We are a true collegium of doctors. We treat chronic patients in a way that corresponds to this vision: that the human body is a temple and that everything that comes from outside must be mastered."

Eve looked at Els and said:

"Could you expand your thinking about what it would mean to start populating such a temple with nanobots? What kind of health would you develop then?"

Els said:

" I have always considered such an idea science fiction, and not to be taken seriously. I never understood how Raymond could. But now that I'm here, as a completely different side of existence is being illumined, I take such a development much more seriously than I did before. I am finding it hard to imagine, that it will ever become a reality to get an injection of nanobots, which then, for example, scour your brain to make observations and work on reverse engineering its processes. Or that they could bring about a major cleansing action of your body, clearing out all the carcinogenic influences: a kind of garbage service by molecular robots! That idea is so fantastical, that you can't imagine that any thoughtful human being would ever really want to hold on to it, and even less that people think there is anyone who might want actually to do this, too."

"Don't be under any illusions about that," said Raymond. "There are large numbers of them!"

Eva said:

"At the beginning of the use of the internet and mobile phones, and later with the internet on mobile phones and air conditioners in hotel rooms and so on, I was terribly troubled by the electromagnetic radiation that all this generates and I also felt that this severely damages your whole system - but at the same time it has a materialising effect. It is becoming more and more difficult to take that other way of thinking seriously. Now we have got used to it over quite a long time, and we notice that materialising, disquieting effect much less. Imagine having billions of these troublemakers in your bloodstream!"

"Again - you'd get used to that … " Raymond retorted.

"Possibly," she said. "But a dramatic materialisation would take place, anyway. That other thinking would vanish over the horizon - like in the evening, when the sun sets and the dusk thickens and the moon rises."

"Artemis," said Raymond.

"I'm having a hard time with her," said Raymond when they went for a walk.

"Why?" said Els. "I really liked what she said!"

"Those stories about angels and hierarchies and the cosmos and the temple … it's all really going too far for me. Johannes limits himself to talking about 'thinking differently'. I can accept that a bit. But this … I don't know how to handle it!"

"I do!" Els said, "I think it all makes sense. But maybe it's going too fast for you?"

As usual, she hit him at the centre of his vulnerable spot. Nothing was ever too fast for him! He thought: I must have time to think it over again!

So, when they were back home he said:

"I need to reconsider all this. A number of ideas have come to me. I would like to explore them further, so that tomorrow, when we get back to Johannes' house, I can ask and say a few things about them."

"We're not going on the internet for hours now, are we?" she said.

"I don't mean that I need the internet for that. I want to consider a few things in myself and then see if, when I re-think it, maybe I can draw it out of it myself."

"Okay!" Els said surprised. "Good!"

So he retreated into the bedroom, sat down in the chair by the window, closed his eyes and asked himself the following question:

In the 2 live contradictions. Now there appear to be two kinds of thinking. One type of thinking is the computational capacity that the human brain has in common with artificial intelligence; the other type of thinking lies in another plane. But when you consider one thought and the other thought, then that means that you set them opposite each other and that they represent opposites, like hot and cold, light and dark, man and woman, et cetera. In those opposites, it is not so that one is right and the other is wrong. From this I derive my question, namely: Shouldn't it actually be so, that this other thinking that Johannes is talking about, is not in opposition to arithmetical thinking, but that it brings balance between this computer thinking on the one hand, and something - which I then wonder what it is - on the other hand? That would then mean that in fact Johannes' thinking represents the 3s, namely the bridging of the opposites and not being one of them.

That's what he was thinking.

He searched in his memory if perhaps there was a third thought, which would have to be in contrast with exact arithmetic thinking. Initially, he would sink into everyday thinking time and time again and his concentration would not be clear and strong enough to keep up with his demands. But by taking himself back again repeatedly, again thinking the question through and again trying to stay with it, he began to succeed in looking around a bit more in the vicinity of the question. And all of a sudden - the answer to that …

He remembered that, when he was still a boy, he had heard a lot about the New Age movement. After the beginning of the new century, the talk about it had been dumbed down. But before the beginning of the new century there was a great expectation that there would be a spiritual renewal. In fact, a similar expectation to that of singularity - only from a spiritual point of view. As far as he was concerned, all this was so vague that he had merely become irritated by it. What Eva had said this morning had a certain resemblance …   … but maybe he did her an injustice, and Els was right with her painful remark that it was all going too fast for him. From his wounded pride, he also drew the strength to concentrate most intensely on this question.

And really, the answer came and he perceived that opposite hard artificial intelligence there is a super-soft mysticism, in which actually no one thinks at all, but in which of course some thinking consciousness must be present. Just as literature and poetry are the counterpoint to arithmetic and mathematics, so mysticism is the counterpoint to AI. He suddenly saw that dreaming of fantasy representations in spirituality is the great counterpoint of hard artificial intelligence! Johannes's 'other thinking' had both the spirituality of mysticism and the exactness of artificial intelligence; and so that 'other thinking' - which was actually a misnomer - belonged to the 3 and was not one of the two 'opposing' forms of thinking!

He felt happy with this insight; it was as if the passage from the 1, which was universal indivisibility, to the 2, which was a total division, had now been enriched and calmed down by the 3 – balancing all opposites.

That, he thought, was an area to which the computer's computing power would never attain. It educated itself within its self-learning element, again and again by choosing between: one and zero; between: yes and no; between opposites: black and white …

The whole world of reconciliation, he now suspected, had to lie outside the reach of the functioning of the computer, and undoubtedly would always lie outside it. The representatives of hard artificial intelligence would certainly - without any foundation, by the way - object: That there comes a time when the computer will achieve that, too … He suspected that this would mean building computers with a heart and not just a brain. But because in hard artificial intelligence, the heart is also assigned to the brain - that could never be the case...

150

The next morning he presented this question and the answer to Johannes and asked him if he had understood it correctly. Johannes listened attentively and after he had finished, Johannes said:

"First of all, you have seen this question correctly and the answer to that question is correct. This is precisely an example for the being of the 3 and I think it's really particularly perceptive of you to have achieved this through your own thinking activity!"

Raymond said:

"Well, of course, I had a bit of help with some information from the Internet. But there I found no question and no answer. Bringing my question together with the meaning of 3, that's really my own invention. That is to say, I had this impression that something just lit up – while I did ask the question with my own thinking, the answer came, more or less, from outside. While it did make use of my existing knowledge, it just structured it in a way that's different from what I'm used to … "

"That's exactly the way it is … " said Johannes. "I wonder, how are you feeling now about the future of singularity?"

"Yes, indeed, that's what I'm mulling over myself … " Raymond said. "I've been thinking and communicating within that community for too long not to know what's going on there. Certain expectations for the future that were very alive at the beginning of the 21st century have not come about. Not when it comes to the timeframe, anyway. But as far as the possibility of realisation is concerned. After all, nanotechnology is now a field of study at university. DNA has been sequenced, as it occurs in the human genome. The technical development of artificial intelligence has taken off, albeit perhaps less than was expected at the beginning of the century. So I don't believe in the time called, 'the 1940s of this century'; nor do I believe in the complete revolution described in singularity. I used to believe in that, but now I see it somewhat differently since I've become acquainted with this other way of thinking, which I perceive now a computer doesn't have. What I used to see as a great expectation for the future, I now see as a very real danger. I would like to warn you against taking this too lightly. It all sounds very fantastic and it looks like science fiction, but Man has a great urge and drive to turn science fiction into scientific reality. With the help of the computer's computational power, science will certainly progress a long way in that direction. You can read articles all the time in the newspaper which state how much people already entrust to the computer. Robots are already being used in surgery. More and more people want to leave the protocols of diagnosis and therapy to the computer to predict on the basis of probabilities how great the chance is that someone has - or will have - this or that. I've always been enamoured with that, Els has always fiercely resisted it. I understand her better now, now that I've sensed the element where that sort of thinking about the 3 takes you. I've also been reminded of Schiller's letters on the aesthetic education of the human being, which I also got to know in the study of philosophy, of course.

"There, a trinity is also described, which may be very different, but not in all respects … One could say that the direction of travel of reason, which has nothing to do with nature, has an affinity with artificial intelligence; and that the direction of travel of nature - the sensory drift, one might say - is that biological sphere which artificial intelligence looks down on. The 'third way' of thinking, then, occupies the area of the urge to play, where the one enters into the other, and the other into the one; which is something that is not a given by nature, but which must constantly arise, because Man himself sets it in motion."

"Boy oh boy!" said Els, "You've taken off!"

Johannes looked a bit startled, but Raymond laughed and said:

"I'm used to hearing that kind of reaction from her! And I can take it from her, too! Yes, I have indeed taken flight - I'm starting to get pretty excited about all this. It's as if an area of desert that had been forgotten about suddenly becomes accessible and fills with scent and colour, with sun and moon also, with stars and planets - not pre-planned at all, but comfortably familiar!"

There was a knock on the door. Johannes got up and said:

"That's Peter!" and called, "Come in!"

A man came in who, in fact, they had already seen, but who now

152

appeared in all his glory. A healthy fifty-year-old with a strong head of black hair with just a trace of grey, almost black eyes and a liveliness and strength that could be disconcerting. During his life, Raymond had always avoided such boys and men. As far as he was concerned, they were too earthy - which his own contemplative nature found hard to cope with. This kind of man, for his part, did not have much sympathy for such types as Raymond.

Now necessity was driving them together and, although Raymond felt some reticence, he gathered himself, stood up and kindly shook hands with the powerful man.

"Come and sit down!" said Johannes. "We've just been having a very interesting conversation - and we're curious to hear what you have to say."

"Yes, as far it concerns me, I'll keep it short. I'm a colleague of Johannes, or rather a student of internal medicine. I worked under his care for a number of years as head of the clinic and when he left he nominated me as his successor - as a professor. But I didn't accept that post, because I wanted to go with him - I couldn't imagine a life without him. And so I retreated to this mountain with him! In the beginning I had some difficulty with that, because of course I had suddenly become a total nobody, I thought. I could cope with a few problems, such as the odd disagreement with Eva and having Johannes and the master get angry with me … . But I also met my great love who I married and have had children with … They were two worlds, and in the end this world triumphed - also because I wanted it to.

"Now Johannes has told me what he's talking to you and Els about. I took the liberty to prepare myself a little bit for this and to delve into it, so I watched a few clips of the great men, the proponents or the initiators of this vision of the future - singularity. And naturally I've read a bit about them as well. Not so much, because what can you take in over a few days?

"But I have to say, the impression I got from these three men: the man of nanotechnology in medicine; the man with the idea of singularity, of the exponential and thought worlds; and the man who originally launched the idea of nanotechnology, who is still alive. I've looked at all three and I have to say I'm stunned at what kind of men they are -"

"Why?" Raymond asked.

"Yeah, I get really angry when I see and hear what they have to say. I'd like to go over there and have a fight with those three! And I don't think any one of them could fight me for more than five seconds … I mean, what a bunch of losers standing there, full of shit! I've been annoyed to death!"

"Take it easy, Peter … " smiled Johannes.

"But apart from the fact that I find it weak, I have some arguments against this whole thing.

"In the first place: what I miss is the evidence of 'practice makes perfect'. As a doctor you know very well that when a muscle is no longer used, it atrophies. This is also the case with the organs. We know that about skills as well. When you haven't practised a certain skill for a long time, it's not completely gone, but not much remains … It is difficult to bring it back up to a level, and then to keep it up with practice.

"How am I to imagine a man, having allowed himself to be infiltrated by artificial intelligence, still being there, as himself?"

Raymond said:

"He doesn't need to be that anymore, because everything artificial intelligence does for him would be much better than anything he could ever do himself. Though I don't support that now."

"But that would mean," Peter said, "that the thinking capacity of biological man becomes totally atrophied and that the moment that happens, he becomes entirely dependent on the activity of artificial intelligence'.

"That has been thought about,' said Raymond, "but it isn't really seen as a problem."

"Well, I do see that as a problem!" said Peter, annoyed. "Here's the next thing: It is clear that all these solutions that this 'venerated' artificial intelligence can offer us are based on calculations of probabilities. I've seen an example of entering data relating to a particular case of illness and how the computer then deals with it. All it can do is put all the details together and say yes or no to each detail and then come to a conclusion with a stated probability. There is no assurance that what you, as a human being, know as a secure intuition, is absolutely out of the question. I've had decades of experience in making diagnoses, and I know: the correct diagnosis always comes as an inner light - not from

154

rehearsing the knowledge you have, but from that knowledge forming itself into the solution. Nobody can tell me that a computer could ever do that.

"It really makes me nauseous when I read how such a program programs itself, how millions of details have been entered and how trial and error - as if it were evolution in a utility shell - leads to the right program for the right question. When you consider how a human being, when he has learned something, knows what it's like in one clear view, then it remains deeply depressing that half the world is in the process of throwing out its divine intelligence in the face of the development of such a stupid thinking-robot - which may seem to come up with great results, but where that intuitive certainty, which plays such a major role for humans, is not present. And then it is promoted to the general public that the computer does have the solutions it comes up with, on the basis of that intuitive certainty - and is not mistaken!

"The example of chess is often used. How the chess computer program can beat the chess world champion, because it can calculate all possible moves and counter-moves in a second and then choose the best move - which the human brain can never compete with. This is put forward as evidence that artificial intelligence would eventually far surpass what a human being is capable of. But what you then forget is, that there is no resemblance at all in the way of thinking about the next step on the chessboard. Of course, the chess player also thinks and wonders what the counter-moves will be if she does this or that. Of course, she can't foresee all possible steps - neither can the computer, but it can sequentially make and calculate them. But what is completely lost from sight is that it is a game, and that it is the joy of the game! A game you have to be able to play correctly, but also to play wrongly. It's not about one sort of perfection fighting with another perfection, because then it doesn't make any sense at all. It is all about enjoying the game.

"Now, I really don't understand anything about this subject - of course I don't know enough about it, and you do, and I'm a person who reacts first and often thinks afterwards: well you could have taken it a bit slower … and now I'm doing it again! But I really don't understand how someone with a fine brain and a pure heart and an energetic enthusiastic will can ever see anything in artificial intelligence that is more than an administrative statistical system."

Raymond nodded and turned pale - while Peter looked even better than when he came in - and said:

"You have an overpowering way of revealing your opinion - "

"It's not an opinion," corrected Peter, "it's a conviction!"

"Good, good," said Raymond. "To reveal your conviction. You do it with so much verve and strength and it's so logical what you say that you carry me with you, too."

"That's good!" Peter said, satisfied, with a smile.

"What it will be like when I get home," said Raymond, "we'll have to see later, but when I listen to you like that … Yes, I absolutely agree with every sentence you say."

"Maybe I'm going too far with this question," said Peter, "but I'm going to ask it anyway - and you'll have to see if you can or even want to answer it! How is it possible that such an intelligent, deep-thinking man like you can get so lost in these ideas of hard artificial intelligence?"

"Well," Raymond said, "Els has badgered me about that many times too, and when I was in no doubt, I was soon done with it, because of course then you know already why you're so passionate about it. Now the question is somewhat different, because I am discovering a different world here, which is not only scientific, too, but which is also purely human. So now - I don't know. That is to say, I do know now, but how it is possible that I gave myself so completely over to arithmetic and how I set aside that overwhelming world of everything else - that is also a growing mystery to me! That's the only answer I have. Maybe later, in the course of time, clarity will come. Right now, I really have no idea….."

They had a chance to talk to Johannes. He said:

"It's not going to be made easy for you. I would have liked to have extended it a bit more, but we only have two weeks."

"I'm going to get all shaken up," Raymond said. "When I can sort it all out for myself later, I'll be able to bear it. But, naturally, the question arises for me: What do you see - or what do you all see - as your task to give artificial intelligence the right counterbalance to this development of the group of scientists?"

"We have some things in common … " said Johannes. "Namely, the desire to understand human intelligence; and secondly, the insight that

156

humanity has entered a phase in evolution in which it is important that it increasingly takes control of further development. It is only by examining the function of the brain and simulating it in devices that the group around hard artificial intelligence is able to fathom this intelligence, and it is precisely in this singularity - in which human beings have invented a machine which will finally initiate a new phase in evolution - that one sees Man taking evolution into his own hands. Man will be populated with micro-devices, the nanobots. Of course, I agree with Peter when he says, that Man will no longer be in the foreground, but will have to step back more or less completely. We, from our different view of Man, see our potential in fathoming intelligence with that very same intelligence, not, therefore, with the help of a device, but with thinking itself; and human thinking can fathom that, because it already knows how it produces its concepts and brings them together in ever-extending knowledge. So much for fathoming intelligence.

"Thus, taking evolution in hand then and there, because the moment you as a human have your own capacity of mental cognition - and can fathom it - from there on, you are able to fathom both inwardly – more and more in yourself and even into the body – as well as outwardly, to fathom nature better and better; with the exclusion of any equipment whatsoever, purely and only on the basis of human thinking itself. But for that it is important that you, as a scientist, make a habit of it, that when you absorb knowledge, you always ask yourself: How did this knowledge come about? Of course, you know better than I do that the results of research on a molecular or atomic level are never direct, but always indirect. There are computer programs interconnected between them. What is actually observed and what humans cannot reach is converted into an observable thing, on the screen. This means that the person who makes that program decides that certain impulses obtained in the research are converted into observable images or text or calculations like this or like that. This means that the 'critique of pure reason', as given by Kant, in which he was obliged to conclude that Man has no control over things, except in mathematics, is becoming more and more a fact, at least in science.

"Man is unable, with his own perception and thinking, to penetrate into what is really happening on an atomic or molecular level. It is converted by a program - with a certain probability - into certain observable representations, into text or calculations, and when you think about it, you can feel how uncertain that science has become as a result. There is an enormous expansion, but the question 'how did this knowledge come about?' should be in your consciousness every time you incorporate research results. Then, of course, your relationship with such research results has become fundamentally different. That doesn't mean that you don't want to record any of it, only that you record it with a certain cautiousness."

"Good." Raymond said. "I can try that. But that's only one side. The other question still remains: How then do I carry out in myself this, let's say, philosophically spiritual reverse engineering of thinking?"

"There," said Johannes, "perception and knowing are one and the same. When you experience this for the first time, it may be the most impressive event of your entire life. You then have the experience that there is something in existence with which you are so connected that there is no limit to what you can know, that there is no abyss between your perception and your understanding, but that it is completely one and the same. That's what Peter was referring to earlier. In that place, there is no calculation of probability, because you are there in the intuitive certainty, that what you think in that self-reflecting thinking is also true. You wouldn't have been able to think it at all if you hadn't first known whether what you are going to think would be true, whether you have yet to discover the truth of it, or whether you know for sure that it isn't true. A whole world is open to you, but it is a world that takes place within, that is also taking place when you are not looking at it. Now you have to look inside and you will have already noticed that it is a messy whole, that inner life of thought, and that it is very difficult to stay focused there. Outside, in the world of nature, things are ordered, even when there is chaos. Inside yourself, chaos always rules, and you have to constantly restore order yourself. That process of inner structuring, so that you create an inner world in which you can then contemplate calmly at a certain moment, that is what we also call meditation. It is annoying that the same word is used in all possible spiritual currents that do not strive for inner clarity. But it's the word that really belongs to this activity, so let's use that designation anyway."

"In the past few days I have had some experience with this and, of course, I still have to get used to the idea that there is even the slightest certainty to be found there. I'm still a long way from the point where I would know that for sure."

"You have to take the right steps methodically to achieve that. We will certainly talk about that after this whole problem of singularity has been highlighted from different angles. Tomorrow I have meetings all day and, unfortunately, I won't be able to keep our daily appointment. I think it's best that we take a day off and that we only continue on Thursday; then we can talk about the 4. I will then ask Beato either to come here for a meeting or we will visit him in his room. I have to see what he would prefer …

"In the meantime: how are you, Els?"

"I love it all!" she beamed. "I feel like I'm getting in touch here with what I'm actually living for, which is what I've always been striving for, but haven't had a framework for it. Now it's all starting to take shape and I think it's really great! Of course, I can see how Raymond has been affected by it and on the one hand of course I wish for that, too; but on the other hand, I am sometimes a bit worried about it. He is a very sensitive person … When the master thunders at him, I do wonder if that's all right … "

Johannes smiled and said:

"I don't believe, as I've said before, that the master would proceed in that way if he wasn't sure that Raymond could bear it, and that it was necessary."

Raymond said nothing.

"Just now," said Els, "Peter was here - and he attacked Raymond in another way - "

"Not Raymond," Johannes interjected, "but the singularity."

" Yes, all right, but he links it all to Raymond anyway. He'll have to deal with that again, in any case. But I'm sure you guys are of the opinion that tough healers are needed."

Raymond still said nothing.

Johannes said:

"Believe me, I have tremendous respect for Raymond, and I know the others do, too. We do perceive his great talent and we also know that we have to respect his freedom. If he wants to stay with the singularity, we will respect him no less for that. But we have a twofold motive to proceed as we do. On the one hand, because it would be better for Raymond himself - let's just say - if he developed a more nuanced view of mankind. But much more importantly, if he, with his background and giftedness, could see that what we are doing here is important, and perhaps even make a contribution to it, then that would have a meaning for the whole world. You may not see it, that this is how things work, but I certainly do see it!

"Raymond is not just anybody. That's why we are all coming to see him, because that's the way it is in fact, and it may seem as if he's being lectured by us, but it's very different in essence."

Raymond put his head in his hands and sighed deeply.

"I'll be all right," he said. "It's unusual, though ... I'm used to being praised - not being treated like this in such different ways. I, too, could hold my head high and ignore everything to save my self-esteem. But that wouldn't be fair to myself either - and I think I always am. I see something now, I'm starting to see something. So I have to press on with that; and I also see how very significant it is that you are putting in so much effort here. Because it has been clear to me from day one, that you are a bunch of giants! I said to Els: We've ended up in Olympus – we've already met Apollo, Zeus and Artemis, and now today Ares as well! I am very curious as to who Beato will be, and then in the final meeting, as to who Philippe turns out to be ... "

Hand in hand they took a walk through the expansive grounds, and then went for lunch in the restaurant. As they sat across from each other Els said, laughing:

"We're already feeling at home here, don't you think? We're even going to have lunch here now!"

"It is indeed a pleasant place, a little aloof from the stresses of everyday life, but not accompanied by those popular nonsensical wellness or sports events ... "

"And how are you feeling, Raymond?"

"You act like I'm a patient who's had an accident and is in recovery, or something! Somehow that's true, of course, but I'd like to uphold my honour a little!"

"I always try," said Els, smiling, "to uphold my patients' honour, too! But perhaps you'd like to answer me?"

"What you said to Johannes, that's right, of course. That oriental mas-

160

ter thundered away at me, even though I was unaware of any guilt. Eva was drawing from some spiritual source with regard to Man. At first, I thought: what nonsense … but it goes on working within you; and then you become a little surprised that over the whole earth, in all universities, there is nothing to be seen of this. And then today: that dynamo … "

Els was laughing.

"Yes, he really is!" Raymond said. "I don't like dealing with men like that. I certainly can't understand someone like that having a wife – because, if I were his wife, I'd be afraid all the time that I'd say something wrong and suffer abuse."

"No! He's not like that at all!" Els said.

"But that's exactly the way he is! However, he must have learned to control himself. You heard that he'd rather challenge those singularity men to a boxing match, to knock some sense into their heads, so they wouldn't think like that in future. On the other hand, of course, he does set things out correctly in a matter-of-fact way. It is so logical, the way he does it, so straight to the point, that if you follow him with good will, you can't help but agree with him. In that sense, it would be interesting to see a two-way conversation between Peter and Kurzweil, for example. But he probably wouldn't listen to him willingly, so that wouldn't work out anyway …

"Yes, Els, these are huge things we're going through here. You say yourself that the furniture in our accommodation looks different every day. So you can work out what effect every conversation here is having! Of course, I feel like I'm being reset. The plug has been pulled out, all processes have been stopped and later, when I have to put the plug in again, I'll have to see what's still in there."

"Usually," said Els, "with such a reset, only the faults go away and the rest just remains."

"Well, I'm meaning a full reset, back to the original settings. I feel something like that. Completely shaken up, completely empty and with very little new perspective - but above all a very great loss of my old perspective. So you feel that you'll have to be strong to deal with that…"

A day off …

They'd got up late and had breakfast. After breakfast, Raymond told Els:

"I'm going to think about all this for a while. It's nice that we now have a day off, so it's possible for me to think through all these conversations. We've had so much to cope with in the past few days and actually hardly any opportunity to put it all in place."

He retreated into the bedroom. As he entered, he saw himself in the mirror on the wardrobe. He stood still … He didn't like looking in the mirror, because what he saw there he didn't find attractive. A young man of medium height, his hair a dark blond and already a bit thin … Light brown eyes behind glasses, an intelligent head, yes, but he had seen more beautiful faces. The posture might be a bit too bent from sitting at the computer all the time. Quite well dressed now, thanks to Els. Actually, an average man, when he compared himself to these Olympic gods he had been with over recent days. There, everyone was individually strong himself. What was he, anyway? Immersed in the image of his special giftedness, absorbed in the incorporation of as much knowledge as possible, living in the hope that this giftedness could be strengthened by an artificial intelligence that had to be multiple times better; and, on the other hand, he lived with Els, whom he loved very much - he, who believed in no soul and who saw the heart merely as a pump to keep the body alive. He had attributed all his emotions and feelings to the nervous system; his head was like an octopus, a very big head with legs that were also nerves … That image probably didn't fit, because an octopus doesn't have a head at all.! But still, he suddenly felt like this: a subject without a heart, but with a need for the storing of knowledge …

He turned away from his reflection and sat down in his chair with some melancholy.

It had started with his wish to write an autobiographical story, but he turned out not to be able to do that at all. Besides, his life wasn't interesting in the least … But by sharing the facts of his development with Els, something had started to happen which, here in the mountains - he smiled to himself – had undergone an exponential acceleration.

Singularity, yes …

All laws, hitherto so strictly defended, had lost their validity here. However, something new had taken their place, something with a new validity.

Oh, he was afraid of death too! And he had consoled himself with the prospect of living ten times as long if technology would take care of his health.

But this new world with its valid laws seemed to bring no consolation for the fear of dying. You had to make the effort to become as strong as possible - in a moral sense, that is - and what that meant for death, he could only suspect at this time. He definitely had to talk to Johannes about death…

Most probably, standing behind that other thinking was a particular certainty of another life, he suspected, and he had sensed that from time to time. But not a word had been spoken about it, and before he went back to Amsterdam that topic would have to be touched on …

He tried to concentrate and recall the conversation with the master. He felt again the impact that that conversation had had on him. But wasn't it true that the master had punished him precisely because of the fact that the proponents of singularity put themselves in the place of God? If the master truly believed in God, it was understandable that he would be filled with wrath over such pride. But for Raymond this was a bridge too far. That other way of thinking - a way of thinking that apparently weaves and lives as meaning in Man - he could sense occasionally, but that of course did not prove at all that that thinking did not come from the brain after all. Nor had it been proved that it belonged to a world that continued to exist when the body is no longer there …

Still, in the moments that he experienced this kind of thinking, he knew for sure that a computer would never be able to simulate it. In doing so, he himself had in fact admitted that one would never be able to find it in the brain.

It might have had something to do with what he remembered from the philosophy of Plato, the eternal Idea. Soon, in his half hour of internet time, he would try to find out about that again, and then include it in his reflections. He remembered that in Plato's philosophy the Idea is seen as eternal and imperishable, of which Man has a part, but which disappears from sight when he walks around in an earthly body.

When he was a student, he had absorbed these thoughts of Plato as beautiful artistic thoughts, without ever thinking that they might be based on anything. Now he thought that Johannes had brought him into contact with that world of the eternal imperishable Idea - in this case the Idea of the 1, the 2 and the 3. The encompassing Idea itself was to be 1, an undivided, all-encompassing, even divine idea. When it passed on to the 2, the idea of the opposition arose, and so on …

He felt again touched by this other thought. It was as if it was looking for him, as if he just had to accept it, and it would come to him.

He was deeply affected by that - but also distracted by it and lost his concentration.

He couldn't see very well how, once back in Amsterdam, he could prepare for his job at the university. Before this trip it had been a natural thing for him. He had his future lectures entirely in his pocket, as it were. Now nothing was right and he really wondered whether he should take up that position. He had already accepted it but, of course, you can always withdraw from something … On the other hand, he felt in himself quite a strong inclination that would most likely make him revert to his old ways again, once in Amsterdam. Maybe all the old would overwhelm the new again? That would be terrible. Maybe he would have to come back here with a certain frequency to immerse himself at the source of his turnaround?

Such thoughts completely confused him again. Every time he encountered such a confusion of feelings and thoughts it seemed to him as if he had lost his trusted mind and, like an infant, had to orientate himself in the world anew. Then he felt strongly: he didn't really want to go back to that 'maturity' he had left behind in Amsterdam.

But Johannes had also said: Just do that for a few years! And actually, most probably that's what he would do….

In the afternoon they went for a walk. The weather was beautiful and thanks to the fact that he had 'lost his mind', his senses were wide open.

He sensed the space from here to the other side of the valley, the space from this height down, the space from this relative depth out into the cosmos. The light illuminated and warmed him. He saw the various trees, the variegated flowers, heard the buzzing of insects, saw his future wife leading the way, cheerful and beautiful as ever … Her senses were, as a gift of nature, open and receptive. She saw and she heard everything and, because of that, she also very delicately observed the states of mind of her fellow human beings. What he overlooked with his thinking, she sensed in the finer points of her fellow Man. He had always thought that it was the price of his thinking, that his sensory perception was not so sharp. But here he began to suspect something of a wholeness, not the eternal distinction between thinkers and doers, but a thinking being active and an active thinking.

The wonderful thing was, that once they were back at the apartment, in his half hour on the internet, while searching for Plato's World of Ideas, he stumbled upon the seven free arts. These were practised by the neoplatonists until the late Middle Ages. He read that they had made a distinction between the alpha and the beta arts: three alpha arts and four beta arts …

Grammar, rhetoric and dialectics on the one hand; arithmetic, geometry, astronomy and music on the other. Johannes had led him with a gentle hand to arithmetic and he suspected that in the quality of this seven – of the three alpha arts and four beta arts - something of what he had felt while walking was to be found: a thinking being active and an active thinking. Tomorrow he would have to ask Johannes about that …

"You're very far away, Raymond," Els said at dinner. " You've forgotten about me, and are lost in your thoughts!"

"In that, my dear Els, you're seeing it all wrong! But when I can't actually live fully in my thoughts, I can't come to terms with myself. I have to rethink all these experiences and try to understand them. That's the only way to move forward and not leave the experiences behind as undigested."

"That is true, but you could tell me about it. "

He told her what he had been thinking that day.

＊

"I haven't reached the 4 yet, Johannes. I had a lot of time to reflect yesterday, and that reflection raised a number of questions. Questions about death, questions about God, questions about Plato's ideas and questions about the seven free arts ... "

"Yes," Johannes said, "we have in fact only talked about thinking because that is the direct counterpart of what is meant by singularity."

"But that," said Raymond, "affects me very much every time I catch a brief glimpse of that other thinking. I wouldn't know why a concept would affect you if there wasn't something else present. Yesterday I was reflecting very deeply about the past few days, and when I think back to Peter's question, how is it that I actually succumb to these views, I think the answer is: fear of death. If I'm honest, I find death an intolerable phenomenon. What you experience in yourself as the essence of existence, your own intelligence and everything you acquire with that intelligence, the people you love and who love you and, finally, your possibilities to contribute something to the world - those three areas you lose when you die. Or rather, you lose everything! You simply no longer exist and that, Johannes, is such an unbearable thought for me, that I am grateful for the men of singularity, who promise me that not too long now - at least within my life expectancy - medicine will be so advanced, thanks to the development of nanotechnology and artificial intelligence, that I won't have to say goodbye at the age of eighty. If there are no accidents, at least, or war breaks out, in a normal life I'll be able to subject myself to a rejuvenation cure again and again with the help of nanotechnology, by which I can extend that farewell to dying for several decades ... Death is an unbearable phenomenon for me."

Johannes looked at him with compassion and said:

"That, my dear Raymond, I can understand very well. I believe that every human being carries that fear in the depths of his being, and I agree with you that many unhealthy, inhuman solutions stem from the desire to escape death. Now there is no escape, and even if you put off the time of a possible death for a few decades each time, that increasingly unbearable phenomenon is still lurking in the distance. Wouldn't it be better to make a reconciliation with death?"

"That would only be possible," said Raymond, "if you could expect death not to be the end of you. In any other case, I don't believe that a reconciliation is possible. But, if in the future it were possible to upload your entire inner life of thought and feeling into the computer, the consciousness you have would become immortal through that device."

"There, Raymond, your intelligent thinking is letting you down! For the fact that you want to live on, is directly related to the fact that you have self-awareness. The animals probably don't have that, they don't have a fear of death. They can't see that somewhere in the future. Death comes and then it's a fact.

"We can see that far ahead because we have self-awareness and that self-awareness brings us the fear that we will one day have to lose ourselves through death. Do you really believe that you could upload that self-awareness onto a computer? That can't be true, that you really think that!"

"It's been predicted!" Raymond objected. "And I'm assuming that, because a lot of previous predictions have come true. I'll think about this later, when I'm home. Whether I could indeed imagine that a computer could also have my self-awareness … "

"What an idiotic idea!" Els retorted. "Surely you know immediately that such a thing is not possible?"

"I can't say that, I don't know immediately! Anyway, let's assume you're right. Then, in fact, for someone who puts everything into this life, on one card, there is no hope of reconciliation with death. Then you come to the existence of, let's say, God, or to the existence of a world that would be a reality outside this physical sensory world. I don't see that world - I don't perceive it and what I hear about it comes to me as pure speculation; like Eva's explanations, with all due respect to her views. It irritates me and makes me feel like I have to listen to something that lacks any foundation."

Johannes said:

"You talk about moments when you catch a glimpse of that other thinking, and it affects you … "

"That's putting it mildly!" Raymond said. "I'm moved to tears…. Are you saying that God touches me there?"

"I'd like to say that," said Johannes, "if I didn't know that such a thing

168

is, for you, pure speculation. So, let me put it another way: Continue your investigations into that other thinking with all your intelligent energy and concentration until God reveals Himself to you. Only then would you know it's not a speculative interpretation - it will be God - but you will be face to face with him and he will tell you who he is. In the meantime, of course, it is not forbidden to read about the experiences of fellow men who have already had such an encounter."

Raymond said, somewhat sceptically:

"You could say that such inner experiences in that other thinking could very well be based on fantasy."

"You might think so," said Johannes, "until you have these experiences yourself. As you know, I am not a fantasy to you now, but the real Johannes with whom you are talking will be just as sure and clear to you when you face the Divine Word."

There was a silence, and it was as if that Divine Word wanted to be present. In any case, Raymond felt the pride of his intellect fading for a moment, he felt somewhat humble, and thought, well, there's a whole world I don't even know about yet.

Johannes said:

"So I advise you not to accept anything at all and to do everything yourself, as if you're an engineer, trying to recreate what others have already found. In your case I think that's quite possible, and that will convince you. I don't want to convince you!"

"That's very clear … " Raymond said. "Now, I have a question about Plato's World of Ideas.

"When I was doing my reflections yesterday, I remembered Plato's theory of ideas. I have the suspicion that this other way of thinking, as we keep on calling it, is directly related to that world of ideas. Could you perhaps say something about that?"

Johannes smiled and said:

"I'd better ask you - if you want to say something about that, you can."

"It will come naturally," said Raymond, "because when I research the 1 and the 2 I end up with Pythagoras and Plato. When I undertake such a thought exercise and briefly illuminate the concept of unity, of 2, and I experience the universal, how big and encompassing such an idea is - even if I only catch a glimpse of it - it reminds me of my philosophy studies. In the beginning we had to immerse ourselves in ancient

Greek philosophy. Of course, I've partly forgotten it, but I remembered that Plato had the conviction - "

"Or maybe he saw it ... "

"Yes, the conviction was that all Man's knowledge is an awakening of what he already has within him as knowledge. If I remember correctly, Plato's world of ideas is a world that was there before you were born and in which you as a human being have been before you were born."

"That's exactly how it is. "

"Any knowledge, anything that is conceptual and glows in thought, would then be a reminder of a pre-birth world, but in a kind of shadow existence. That is the famous allegory of Plato's cave, which he pictured in that significant work 'The State'. That would mean, if Plato's conviction is based on truth: that we as human beings were already there before we were born. Then, of course, it is obvious that you will still be there after death. Then the earth would exist like a railway station where you get off for a little while and then move on again. Then, too, death could lose much of its frightening effect, although it is probably always painful when you get back on the train and leave the station, and say goodbye to all your loved ones who are remaining there on the platform. I've always found that so difficult. The question then is: How can you strengthen the awareness of that world of the Idea in such a way that it becomes reality for you, and get rid of that shadow existence of the Idea, as it were? By remembering the heavenly, in life on earth: then death would become something acceptable.

"But the question remains: Why is death really necessary?"

"To that question," Johannes said, "there are, of course, many answers. The closest answer is that the human world is not exactly a perfect one. We humans, among ourselves, will endure with each other for a while, but not forever in the same way. You can see that when people grow too old, they occupy a position that could be freed up for the younger generation - that can sometimes be very beneficial.

"But if you imagine that this life was to be artificially stretched to infinity, then the whole of human development would be stopped, as it were, because you would have to continue with a bunch of imperfect people, who wouldn't develop any further either, because they themselves would become less and less active. They would have been able to derive their intellectual capacity from a machine, and their health from a machine."

"That sort of thing is not really talked about. People are longing for an extension of life - what that means in the big picture, I haven't really heard enough ideas about that. For development, dying down and re-building anew is necessary – that's how nature is sustained."

"So the question is: How can I give this world of ideas a certain resilience?"

"There were well-defined ideas about this in Plato's school. In his work on the State, Plato poses the question: What 'subjects of learning' could lead to the soul being led from the shadows into broad daylight and ascending to being real? That is exactly your own question. His answer is: arithmetic, geometry, astronomy and music. And when the alpha subjects are developed in addition, then we can unite both branches of knowledge - which is the same as the search for harmony, the search for the ideal of universality. For us in these modern times that means: by contemplation in pure thinking - that other thinking - to really experience the Idea and then to unite it with creative living that then focuses on that inner process of forming thought."

"I was thinking yesterday," Raymond said, "in reality it is a search for the will in thinking and thinking in the will. That occurred to me, although I have no idea how you'd develop that."

"I hope," Johannes said, "that in the next few days, at least as far as the method is concerned, that will become clear to you, so that when you are at home you can develop this further."

"I am not looking forward to going home at all … " Raymond admitted. "I feel very well here with you and I am afraid that if I return to my old life, in my old environment, the 'disease' will strike again."

"I don't think so!" said Johannes. "Not only have you gained an insight here, but that insight has completely changed you. An insight one can forget; but a total change carries on working even when you're not aware of it anymore. We will consider at the end of our series of meetings whether and how we could continue with these meetings."

Els had kept silent most of the time, but now she said:

" Why is it, Johannes, that you and your colleagues are trying so hard to help us on our way?"

Johannes looked her straight in the eye and said:

" It depends on who you are!"

Els had thought of the Labyrinth again that night - whether it was a dream or a waking thought, she could no longer tell. She saw how the monster was hiding. It was far from being conquered …

Beato came to Johannes's room for their conversation. Els and Raymond hadn't met him yet. He seemed to be in his forties and was possibly the handsomest man in the place. After they had greeted each other and introduced themselves, they sat down again and Beato began:

"I was born in Italy, in South Tyrol, and grew up with German as my mother tongue. But I also speak English well, so maybe it would be easier to communicate in English?"

Raymond said:

"We can both understand German very well, although speaking it is something else. But let's try!"

'Well … " Beato said and he continued in German.

"I met Johannes at a congress in Leiden where we were both present and, as you will understand, I also am a doctor … I qualified as a surgeon and specialised in the more difficult field of trauma surgery. I still practise that, three days a week, in Milan. The rest of the time I am here, trying to contribute to the work that is going on here. I returned again last night, but I had already heard you were here and I was able to prepare myself a little bit for this theme.

"I think it's an extremely interesting area … "

Raymond looked surprised.

"Yes really!" he said. "It is quite understandable that when you have no religious background and you have grown up in physics and abstract scientific thinking, this fascinates you - and I think it is mainly because it is, after all, half way true. That is to say, it may be wholly true in itself, but the half that is missing is that other thinking and the whole world that is related to that.

"So, at best it is half true, because the other half has been omitted. When I take a more or less global view of singularity, the striking thing is, of course, that intelligence is estimated here as the most important object in evolution, and that it is rightly felt that a new developmental impulse is needed. And because that appeals to what every human being knows deep inside himself, you can easily get enthusiastic about it. I can understand that very well. We really are at a point of development where intelligence has to go through a renewal. That is entirely correct. So, when you have nothing else at your disposal but abstract human intelligence and what the computer can add to that, then it is understandable that one hopes to achieve a renewal that way. How attainable that really is remains to be seen, but technology will progress a long way. Of course, we are already living with artificial intelligence – by leaving elements of our difficult work to it. When I have to write a patient's letter of discharge, I simply dictate it into my iPhone with a certain app and the letter writes itself out. That's just one example. If I want to know something about singularity – yes, you know how it is - just type in the word and you'll get a whole series of articles and websites and books with information about it. Man's dream of having all-encompassing knowledge is quite understandable. I remember stories from the late nineteenth century in Vienna about a man, Friedrich Eckstein, who they called MacEck. It was said of him: when you don't know something, just ask him, he knows everything. He was like a kind of living internet that you could consult. As a joke, it was said that even the encyclopaedia came out of the bookcase to ask him for advice … !

"Now, everyone has access to it. Of course, these are great things! Also, the possibilities of communication across the globe … I don't think you should simply be critical of that. I, at least, am making grateful use of it. We also have certain equipment in surgery to perform complicated operations, using a so-called robot. That takes some getting used to, because you're no longer working directly on the patient's body with your hands, there's something in between. But if that is much better and more effective than the clumsy, vibrating hand of a human being, why not use it?

"In this desire to develop, eventually, such a powerful and high-speed artificial intelligence that can fill the whole cosmos and even penetrate into other galaxies, something arises in which you can start to see who is actually putting his signature on it … . When mankind still had spiritual wisdom, it was known that the whole cosmos is filled with cosmic intelligence, that there are forces at work there that are intelligent, so the planets have the particular orbit that they have and the relations between the different celestial bodies are precisely as they are. Also, that what is present on earth as the natural kingdoms is thought and shaped by cosmic intelligence. We have always called the cosmic intelligence that formed, and continues to form the cosmos, and also the earth: the

'Holy Spirit'. It was imagined - and these representations are still based on a visionary view - that there is a high spiritual being who is, as it were, in control of this cosmic intelligence. You see him everywhere in images like the archangel Michael, who fights - and conquers - the dragon.

"Of course, it is actually impossible to put into words such a great cosmic and earthly development within half an hour. But I want to say something about it, and that is: that cosmic intelligence, which is thus active everywhere, so that things can function harmoniously with each other according to the law of the present, has gradually become, more and more, after the coming of Christ, the intelligence of mankind. So imagine: the whole organization of creation appears as an extract in everyone's human intelligence. When you know that, it is of course bizarre to think that Man with his intelligence should enrich it with a device, then repeat the divine work and give it back – digitized and mechanized - to the cosmos what he carries within him as a gift from the cosmos itself.

"And yet there is a kernel of truth in it! A human being must indeed come to know that what lives in him as human intelligence has once been cosmic intelligence – and know it so thoroughly that he voluntarily reconnects it to the cosmos.

"So: in itself, the thought of that process is not bizarre; only the interconnectedness of a device makes it into something - excuse me for saying it - devilish, satanic even.

"What would happen, if what the people of singularity hope for were to come about? A mechanical, digitally intelligent humanity, in which the biological becomes inferior. At the same time, the connection with the real activity of the Holy Spirit would be cut off, which would mean that the earth - with the cosmos, in so far as it, too, had isolated itself with artificial intelligence - would become detached from the living tree of creation. An exclusion would arise that would try to maintain itself on the basis of technology. On the contrary, something completely different must happen! We can learn to transform in ourselves what we know as an abstract intellect into a spiritual intelligence: we can find spirituality in it. Then we can strengthen it and give it back to the Cosmos, which would then give new life. In that way earth does not become detached from the tree of creation as a useless fruit. But on the

174

contrary, earth would have the power to connect spirituality in a new form with the cosmos.

"Indeed, Man will carry intelligence upward through the universe, not through hard artificial intelligence, but through intelligence that reconnects with its original spirituality. There is a fashionable expression, which is used to indicate that something that is recognized does not provide the full extent, the total knowledge, the ideal solution. It is then said: Of course, this is not the Holy Grail!

"When abstract human intelligence, which is indeed imperfect, manages to awaken spirituality within it, then the Holy Spirit comes and enlivens all of the dead knowledge in Man. That is the Holy Grail! Nothing will be lacking there. In this way the veil between death and life will be lifted. Not as early as 2040; it will take much, much longer. But the beginning of that transformation starts now!

"Once again, you don't have to give up the kernel of this idea of singularity. All you have to do is find another shell."

Beato remained silent and it was obvious that this speech had cost him a lot of strength.

Raymond was deeply moved. This man showed him understanding, no reproaches, no antipathy. He had accepted him with the full sympathy of an understanding fellow human being.

Beato said:

"Reading all that information about the anticipated singularity, I was impressed by the enormous amount of energy they have put into propagating this vision. And I do wonder, Johannes: Is what we are doing here sufficient counterbalance? Shouldn't we be applying even more precisely, even more intensively, an increasing amount of power and energy to bring the spiritualization of thinking into our culture, and to propagate it?" Johannes nodded and said:

"I think so, too. That is the good thing about becoming so familiar with this impulse of singularity, that you feel, as it were, how intellectually-driven it is. And then, of course, what is storing and transmitting all this information is the electromagnetic field, which we know makes the development of any thinking other than the abstract very, very difficult. When the technical development of artificial intelligence grows exponentially, then the resistance to, and the difficulty of spiritual thinking also grows exponentially."

"Until then," Beato said, "you know how to take the step out of that whole material realm, and then you can easily find the original light and elasticity and form-giving capacity of real thinking."

Raymond said:

"Well then, *that* is what has to be learned! How, with my consciousness, do I step outside that electromagnetic field in which you think we are enmeshed?"

"The problem is the addiction to the content. It would be good if you read the story of Wolfram von Eschenbach, Parzival … "

"I know that story," Raymond interrupted, "from Wagner's opera."

"Then you could try to feel how Amfortas is an image for the addiction to the world - and in the inner life of thought that is the addiction to knowledge - as many facts, facts, facts as possible! Parzival, on the other hand, is the primal image of knowing how to find - how to get in touch with - the Holy Spirit. Then, of course, you have to regain the content, or you have to spiritualize the existing content. But there is a doorway. There, you must be able to renounce all content. This is so difficult because the Internet loves billions of facts, and we are so accustomed to that."

"In theory I can understand … " Raymond said. "But how that should be put into practice is a complete mystery to me."

Johannes said:

"You still haven't met one of our people here - Philippe. We saved him for last! I expect he will be able to make clear to you what you could do to switch away from that concept of singularity to the spiritual intelligence that comes from the stars, and returns there … "

"What do you think about all this?" Els asked Raymond at lunch.

"Beato really is a very nice man. If only they were all so kind!"

"I don't think that would have had any impact? A 'reset' means that you undo everything that's already set, all in one go, right? I think that was the master's impact."

Raymond shook his head and said:

"Actually, it was Johannes's first lecture. There, I already had the feeling of being completely shaken up, because something is being addressed that you know to be true, even if it contradicts everything you have become deeply attached to … "

"But what do you think of it?" Els repeated.

"What I am saying is: I am getting to know something here that I was completely unaware of, although I have to admit that I know – spontaneously - that it is true! That in itself is quite extraordinary, I'm sure not everyone experiences that. For me, there is no doubt about it. This is true. But this truth completely undermines my previously carefully constructed truth - and I do feel resistance to that, I think that is understandable…"

"That's certainly understandable," said Els, "but not very productive. What's the point of resisting a truth that you yourself acknowledge?"

"It may not make sense," he said, "but it does work. It even hurts in a way, also because I have to admit that I was probably on the wrong track with my own knowledge, which I thought was true. I don't think anyone likes to admit that."

"On the other hand," she said, "it's a proof of greatness if you can admit it! But, what do you really think?" she asked for the third time.

"I don't know what you want to hear, Els! I feel confused, and it will be some time before I've cleared up that confusion. I have already asked Johannes a couple of times: Show me a secure way to get home to that other element of thinking - and so far I haven't really got a clear answer."

"Except," said Els, "that today he did say: We saved Philippe to last! I heard in that answer that he's going to give you some directions as to which path to take. Or rather, which way *we* should go, he will give *us* directions. For, as you'd expect, it is equally true of me that I would like to become familiar with that other element of thinking."

"Definitely," he said, "I always think of us together! But you already had serious reservations about the singularity, while I did not. So, in that sense there's a big difference. I'm having to make a tremendous turnaround and I feel it's very, very difficult - although I do recognise it."

"So it comes down to a test of your sense of truth," Els said with her innate wisdom. "So now you have, more or less, to put what you embrace abstractly in second place to something that you know for sure is true, but can't imagine abstractly… That's quite something!"

He said:

" Yes, and I'm really suffering with that; which is nonsensical - because why not welcome real truth with joy?"

"That's probably mainly because it makes you feel ridiculous … "

Raymond nodded and remained silent, and then said:

"The problem with the vision here is that although you know it's true, you can't really get your hands on anything that could help explain it to someone else. That's what makes it so intangible and certainly not describable. It is a kind of conversion. And because you're used to being able to describe everything - even if it's probabilities and not certainties…. I'll also find it hard to say goodbye to the fresh mountain air again. At first, I was locked in a virtual world and when we came here it was a totally strange environment for me, this world full of fresh sensory impressions. Now I have become somewhat accustomed to it and am now having to give up this natural world, as it were, for a spiritual world."

"That task seems to me to be less all-encompassing and definitive than what you had imagined with regard to singularity - in which the whole of nature and biology was, in the end, to give way to a technologically virtual world! Life would then have become one big computer game - which might even be a wonderful ideal prospect for many people …

"When you have to give up nature for the sake of the mind, I believe that that only applies at certain moments, and that for the rest of the time you can enjoy an ever more intense experience of nature. That's what I feel, only I can't prove it … "

" I am very low anyway," Raymond said. "Everything is in jeopardy, and I hope that you will continue to monitor the process so that I don't slip back, from feelings of misfortune, into that future vision of a technological virtual world."

"That is indeed a danger … " she said. "It reminds me of a summer romance. When you meet one another in those ideal circumstances and spend some time together really enjoying the holiday, it seems as if you will never forget it and you will spend the rest of your lives together. But then you go home and everything is the way it was, and so is the other person. But most often, one of them views the whole thing as a castle in the air and doesn't respond anymore …

"You come across a completely different vision of life in this place and you feel the dedication given to it. But once you are back home in your humdrum ordinary circumstances, in a street with high-rise housing, never-ending stairs, where a lot of people live, where the computer is

178

sitting on your desk, and so on … ”

"I'm very curious who Philippe is," Raymond said. "We must have seen him but I haven't really noticed him, because in the meantime we've been meeting everyone I did notice."

"There was a man with a very beautiful woman - they were also in the front row. An unremarkable man, with a striking woman, I remember that," said Els.

The next morning Johannes took them directly to Philippe's room and accompanied them inside.

When he saw him, he did recognize him, after all. He had indeed seen him on both of the lecture evenings, but had not identified him as a special person.

Raymond was too nervous to take in any details; he gradually calmed down during the conversation and saw what kind of man he actually had in front of him. Outwardly, he seemed the essence of silence, all quiet, silently motionless, friendly.

But when he spoke, the impression he made changed completely. It was as if he shifted into a state of spiritual rapture, while he himself remained calm and his intellect worked normally.

He spoke slowly and deliberately, but you felt a tremendous enthusiasm in him. He introduced himself as follows:

"My name is Philippe Laurent … My mother was Dutch, my father a real Frenchman. I grew up in the Netherlands because my father had a job at the university as a philosopher. I got to know Johannes in college, when he was a professor there and I was working as an assistant. He himself asked me to become his assistant, but I didn't fancy it. I worked as a general practitioner for a while and after that I went more in a literary direction. The contact with Johannes was renewed because, when I had a magazine and was living in Paris, I was asked to translate his books into French - which I did. At the same time, I was becoming proficient in meditation, in the development of that other way of thinking.

"That thinking becomes, as it were, a new dwelling place, from where one can get to know both the cosmos and the microcosm - the body.

"I met my wife Angelique during my studies and she became a general practitioner and eventually, when we moved here, took up a position as a colleague of Eva. We don't live on the grounds but lower down in the town.

"Like all the others, I have immersed myself as well as I could in this vision of singularity, in just a few days. It was not unknown to me, but

I never met anyone who was really part of that group. In that sense, it really is an honour to meet you!

"I believe that the most important argument is that the whole of technological development takes place through Moore's law, the law of the exponential growth of technology. He talked about transistors and his law reads: The number of transistors in an integrated circuit doubles every two years because of technological progress. At a certain stage, a point would be reached at which, beyond all the steady growth, the increase would rise almost straight up on a graph and would then actually no longer be achievable with human intelligence. Human beings would then have to accept the help of technology in order to keep up with this whole development. Moore talked about transistors in an integrated circuit; by others this has been extended to the doubling of the technical results in general, and so also with regard to artificial intelligence.

"When I let my reading on the internet take effect on me - I've also read quite a bit in Kurzweil's thick book – I get the impression that there does at first indeed appear to be an exponential growth in this development, but that in the end this doesn't follow through, in fact. Moore himself has actually retracted his law, in the sense that he thinks it's of limited duration (2006), but his followers hold on to it. There is talk of a decline since 2011.

"One can see that the reports about the results of technological development in the fields of nanotechnology, gene technology and robot technology are optimistic and positive, but no longer indicate that what the singularity followers hope for, will soon become fact. I believe that the more moderate people are, by now, really doubting this. Over the last few years there have also been fewer publications. I have read that the initiator of the EU Human Brain Project has now identified 31,000 cells of a rat brain, but it has to be admitted that the human brain - if I remember correctly - has 100 billion cells. If that has to be 'captured' in this way, I'd say it's an infinite process … "

Raymond objected:

"That's what was thought when DNA was identified, until a method was found which now makes sequencing DNA a simple laboratory operation."

"That could be," Philippe said. "But it could just as well be that an equivalent short circuit like that isn't found. In any case, there's no clear view as yet of such a revolution. I actually mean more the 'general atmosphere' one notices, the experience one gets, when one immerses oneself in the literature. Not that the enthusiasm has cooled down, but the facts speak for themselves - that things are not going so fast after all. I think that a lot of Kurzweil's dizzying predictions are not going to come true and that when he is seventy, eighty, ninety, maybe a hundred-years-old, he'll just have to die, anyway. He can still freeze himself in liquid nitrogen in the hope that he can be resurrected by the time the technology is ready. But he'll have to say goodbye to this earth's existence.

"The thoughts of people like Kurzweil and Freitas are daring - and blasphemous for a man like me. When one can look forward to the fact that Man will no longer need a heart in the future because small devices can circulate in the blood circulation - while there will also be no more blood: which takes care of the oxygen, breathing and cleaning up the waste - then one is acting very strangely. If one absorbs such thoughts, which have the appearance of fantasy on the one hand, one then has a fearful suspicion on the other hand that there is an element of reality behind it. Probably the others have already told you about that, perhaps in a different way.

"In any case, it makes it clear to me how important it is, not only to find that other thinking, but also to present spiritual knowledge of the human body in contrast to this technological representation of the body. Biology is seen as a tricky area that is imperfect and that would be better perfected with technical equipment. Spiritual knowledge of the human body would clarify that such a non-biological body already exists. It does not need to be conceived and constructed at all, it has been present since the year 33 of our era; and it is through inner development that one can acknowledge the presence of that body. By getting to know that body, one absorbs its seed and experiences how it can grow into the hereditary body, as it were, so that one may hope that when one dies - now or next time - not only does one shed the mortal body and merge into a spiritual existence, but that one can resurrect into that other body that has to do with that other thinking."

Raymond said:

"That sounds as fantastic to me as the vision of singularity."

"The difference is," said Philip calmly, "that this fantastic representation can be proven as truth within yourself, leaving no point of doubt, simply because you begin to sense that body within yourself, just as you began to sense that other thinking within yourself, earlier. Then perhaps you can imagine in your mind that, if that were true, it would be possible that this other thinking is the consciousness of that other body and that it, indeed, has eternal life."

"And is that not Teilhard de Chardin's vision?" Raymond asked.

"No not at all; he posits, as in singularity, a technical electromagnetic representation of an eternal body, which is one for all human beings; while the reality of that spiritual body is that it has no connection whatsoever with physical existence - with material existence, I should say, for it *is* a physical body, but *is not* material: it has everything the people of singularity imagine that their 'Cyborg' body will ever have - only then in the full glory of the totality of spiritual existence that is interwoven with soul and permeated with life.

"That body will not have a virtual existence, but an existence in a reality as intensely present as you experience now only in moments of the most intense love."

Raymond felt a kind of guilt rising up inside him and he didn't know where to look.

"But Philippe, where is the point of connection between our material existence and our everyday consciousness? In singularity it is already clear: it is artificial intelligence. What is the starting point in your vision, and how do you cultivate it in such a way that what you paint as a vision of the future can actually come about?"

"Look" said Philip, "it seems to be an unequal battle and maybe it is. Even though the majority of scientists are probably sceptical about the singularity, in part this mixing of man and machine will certainly be pursued and, possibly, eventually achieved. There are hundreds, maybe even thousands of scientists actively working on it, much capital is being invested in it, and the status one can derive from it is not insignificant, either. On the other hand, there is a handful of people who are undertaking their work more or less in secret, who are not active on the big world stage and who generally have no money and no possibility of getting funding. Of course, it is also correct to observe that the money is in the hands of those working on an external manifestation of singularity and so, naturally, no money is made available for an inner manifestation.

"Moreover, at the outset, one is reaching into nothingness, while in the scientific work one finds a very extensive field. And even if, in the inner life of many people, we succeeded in arriving at a point of view there, every participant who joined us would have to work within himself, in order to awaken that field of research - which would also then become that new body. By its own nature, it remains imperceptible.

"But your question is: what does one have to do in order to strengthen, stabilize, make powerful what one sometimes feels very delicately in one's thinking – that a corner of the veil covering that other thinking is lifted slightly - so that one can undertake one's own research there and discover for oneself, that what we are saying here is based on, and is indeed, reality.

"I'm going to need a few words to be able to express that fully. In itself, this idea is not at all new. Aristotle had already become conscious of the category of substance in describing the foundations of his logic. One can give a detailed philosophical reasoning about that, but one can also say: in the separate thing one is facing through perception, one is observing by thinking that it *is*. Determining the being of a thing in the outside world goes at first unnoticed: its certainty, a kind of first orientation that is of fundamental significance. Kant, later on, shook up such certainty, but one can get back to it. It takes some effort, but one has to focus again and again on the things and the people around one, and ask oneself the question: *is* this real? Establishing the *being* of an individual object is an act of knowing, one might say, which one carries out continuously, without however being aware of it. It is too obvious to constantly think about it. If one does this on a regular basis, one soon begins to distinguish between what makes a positive impression of *being*, and where that is less clear or not at all the case.

"When one focuses on the meaning of 1, as you did with Johannes, one finds that 1 *exists* in a different way than when one focuses on the being of Els, for example, or of this table.

"The next step is to go inside and wonder to what extent one recognizes oneself as *being object or subject. Am I* a reality, as this table really is? What is the experience within oneself, of recognizing that one is there? This is a level of being that a human being thinks much less about, because as soon as one does this, one is confronted with the possibility of possibly *not being there ever again*. It makes one immediately aware

185

of the finiteness of one's existence and that is why one prefers not to go there.

"And yet, it is precisely at this point, that that world of other thinking, of that other acting, begins to reveal itself.

"If one pays close attention when one does that, then one will be able to discern oneself both in an 'I' that is more of an abstract deduction and in a *real* 'I' in which one becomes aware that one is really there at that moment.

"The *I am* from the inference is the ordinary every-day I-awareness that knows about being there, but doesn't immediately sense it. One concludes that one is there."

"Yes," said Raymond, "the way I've come to know the *I am* it is the sum total of all the processes of physical consciousness."

"But you see," said Philippe, "that's an inference. The perception that one is there could be correct, but it's also possible that it comes from a very different source: it is an abstract conclusion. And yet one is sure that one is there. One can also look at one's biography and conclude from that biography that one is there. When one delves into this, one will notice that the main component of *I am* consists of a kind of looking in a mirror and seeing something that is certain, but the origin of it one doesn't really know yet. With that *I am* one doesn't really get any further. When one compares it with the table that is there, one can also conclude that, on the basis of data from one's perceptions, it must be that there is indeed something there.

"But one has to go deeper. One can really sense the presence of the table. One can also go that deep with oneself. It is much easier than with the table, but as I said, it is also much more threatening than with the table, because there one touches on the possibility that the table's existence is finite; that, at most, is a pity; but that one's own self should have an existence that is finite – well, that is the greatest drama that exists.

"And yet, when one has the courage to penetrate into this awareness of the self in the depths, where one knows for sure that *one is there*, then at the same time the portal opens back to one's birth, as does the gate forward to existence after death. One feels that *the being of the self* cannot be temporal. It is as if one would want to mark a piece of the infinite ocean and say: only this exists and I don't believe in the rest. With this truly deep *I am*, one senses the whole ocean of existence, the totality of eternity, however much one certainly cannot comprehend right away. But one gets an experience of eternity in this *I am* and that is a point that is fairly easy to reach if one really has the courage to do so. It cannot be touched by electromagnetic radiation or artificial intelligence or whatever. It's like a magic word, but one has to do it right.

"You might very well try this tonight and then come back to me tomorrow and say: 'It's not true at all, what you've told me. Because I won't reach it and even if I do reach it, then I won't be sure - and I'm constantly being distracted by all kinds of other thoughts.'

"It's not that simple, but it's all about *the core of the experience of being* that has to do with physical existence in the first place. But you soon experience that this physical existence does not define the boundaries of this experience of being, that it radiates around and reaches out. So pay close attention: it's all about *being*."

Raymond had listened intently and now said;

"This reminds me of Fichte. I thought this was an interesting philosophy, but then ignored it as obsolete. Isn't it true that he also speaks of 'positing the self'?"

"Yes," said Philippe, "that's how it is … But this reaches further. Here one really has to concentrate on the search for being, and when one's found it, one's found the spirit of the human being, as the spirit has a body. There are many visual descriptions of it. The most famous one, I think, is the New Jerusalem. That's an image, of course. And that is very hard to accept for the man of today, with his intellect. But when one keeps in mind that this is the body that will arise in future, one can find comfort in it.

"But between the step of becoming aware of the being of one's self and the full glory of the New Jerusalem, there is still a long, long period of development."

"How do I know," Raymond asked, "that it is the *real being of my self* that I then sense? I could imagine that in my ordinary body perception I also have a kind of I experience. I might perceive that for the true experience of being, which is a completely different experience of being, it seems to me."

"That's right," said Philippe. "One always has to keep in mind that in that other thinking the self has existence. That's where one can get to know and find it, not in the dull feeling of *being the self* that exists naturally.

"So, one has to elevate oneself to the development of pure non-sensory, non-personal thoughts and then ask oneself the question: Am I?"

"I don't think it's that simple after all … " Raymond said, hesitantly.

"But it is simple, in the sense that it is a point you are looking for - and not a whole world of unknown impressions. For the scientist, there is another access that can help find this point; whereas you can go to the boundary of knowing. The modern scientist tends not to see boundaries or set boundaries everywhere. But you can also take a concept of which you know the meaning but of which you do not know the reality. For example, understanding power. You can think of that concept physically and then come to the conclusion that you do not yet feel 'force' with that concept; that you actually do not really know what power is, although you can express and calculate it in formulas, draw vectors etcetera. When you can balance in that point of transition from everything you know, to that realization of not knowing reality - then you achieve balance in *the self*. That can't be the being of the body, because you're thinking in a field where that body isn't active. If you can develop an experience of being on that boundary, then you know for sure that this is the *true I am*."

"It's hard to get a hold of this … " he said. "You're handing me something – with nothing to hold on to … !"

"Well, of course, you can't - with an area that isn't tangible. But you can follow these clues, and I expect it won't take too long before you'll have significant sensations in the process."

"I'll have to let it sink in, at least; and then apply it … " said Raymond. "But now, I'm feeling as though I've completely lost my mind!"

Philippe laughed, and said:

"That's fair enough, because at this stage, where I'm taking you now, the mind has very little to contribute, and there's another thinking that's going to work. That is the *I as an action*: no longer as a sequence of thoughts, but as a sequence of actions."

"I'm getting rather despondent … " said Raymond. "Surely you can't expect this to counterbalance the enormous development of artificial intelligence?"

"You underestimate the reality of the world of the Idea. It exists, and everything that the men and women developing artificial intelligence are trying to discover has long been known in that world. Little by little, they lift up a few threads of the veil. I tell you, Raymond, if you get to that point and you hold your ground *in being you*, I can tell you that you will not be lifting a few threads of the veil there, but that the whole veil will be lifted, and that you will face wisdom itself: which encompasses everything."

"I still have a question," Raymond said. "What I don't understand is how such a completely subjective, non-scientific experience of the self could ever resemble the result of scientific research on the brain and related reverse engineering of the brain. It seems completely irrational, doesn't it?"

"That's an understandable question," said Philip calmly, although he sensed a slightly mocking tone in Raymond's manner of speaking. "Artificial intelligence, as a science, is looking for a specific algorithm of the individual human brain, so that with this algorithm the whole size and meaning of the individual brain could be uploaded back into a computer. That would mean that you could preserve your specific nature, as far as it is related to brain activity, in a machine. That program would then continue to work even after your body died. Am I expressing that correctly?"

Raymond nodded.

"That's consistent with the idea of DNA as some kind of algorithm for the functioning of the human body. There is a tendency in Man to want to store, hold and acknowledge everything in a formula. With this, however, both the brain and the DNA correspond to a certain inner quality of the human being, in whom all this is already present in all its finesse and detail. I have called this 'the self' in my presentation today. That is a somewhat questionable use of the term, because philosophically and psychologically there are many interpretations of 'the self'; also, from a scientific point of view one can go in many directions with it - you have already mentioned one and we could add many more. So, one really should have another designation. But what I'm aiming for is the certainty that you, as an intelligent thinking human being, exist within that intelligent thinking. You do that in a very special, individual way, which you would like to upload. Similarly, I do that too - in a very different, special, individual way. Although in our thinking we deal with the so-called universalia - i.e. with the concepts that are in themselves equal for all people - we each deal with these general concepts in a completely individual way.

"Artificial intelligence searches for a formula, an algorithm, to establish that. Kurzweil has discovered - and he will not be the only one - that the recognition of thought patterns plays an important role in this. Those patterns are sought out, and so one reveals the potential of recording the peculiarities of the functioning of a brain. But when one goes into these things from the other way of thinking, one sees that what the brain allows itself to perceive is in fact nothing more than a reflection, a conversion into electricity in a very special way, of something infinitely more differentiated and rich. But the totality of that differentiated, rich, inner individual existence can also be summed up in one point. Only then one doesn't call it an algorithm - I call it, for convenience now, *'I am'*. We have a universal name for ourselves, namely 'I', but the activity of that 'I' is individually different, specific, unique. One can learn to draw attention to that *I.* One can become at home in one's own intelligent functioning, one can also apply a kind of reverse engineering, by deliberately imitating what one discovers in it. Humanity's problem is that everyone wastes most of their waking life on useless thoughts and feelings. That is what artificial intelligence wants to maximize. But that would take away from that point that one could call *I,* from becoming aware of the diversity and specificity within oneself.

"Certainly, there is a pattern, there are multiple patterns and those multiple patterns coincide, as it were, in a grand life pattern. But we only have a vague impression of this in our consciousness, and we call that impression: 'I'.

"I want to tell you, Raymond, the true 'algorithm' of your human being is an 'algorithm' that has meaning not merely for thinking, but for your whole being in this life - and even for your being in many other lives and in many future lives. That 'algorithm' refers to all that - but I'm putting it in quotation marks, because it is not a formula based on calculation.

"You have been assessed as a gifted child from your earliest childhood. That means that you have an intelligence that is so fast and profound that you distinguish yourself from your fellow human beings. Once you suspect *who it is*, who is using and enriching that intelligence, you will get a glimpse of immortality. The body, then, is just a cloak that you have put on and that you take off at the end of your life to prepare for a new cloak … "

Raymond asked:

"Does that mean that the way I have to deal with intelligence is always the same?"

"Not quite … " said Philippe. "The giftedness that you have in this life also stems, of course, from the physical existence that you have been given, also on the basis of heredity. Certainly, you need a 'reflector' that does a good job, in order to make what you are capable of in life on earth a reality. The quality of your body next time, and what parents you get, for example, will depend on how you work morally during this lifetime. It could be that next time your way of dealing with intelligence would be confronted with a body that masks it and makes it dull, and then you would not be as intelligent. That would be a very great suffering."

"So how am I supposed to do this?" Raymond asked, any mocking tone having by now disappeared. "How am I supposed to bring clarity to what is dull and subjective, yet at the same time so all-encompassing, and that corresponds to the exactness of an algorithm?"

"Well," said Philippe, "I can't give you a magic formula! This is indeed a task and, depending on your past history, it will take you a shorter or longer time to shed some light on that general feeling of being in one's thinking. It's hard work and it's work in solitude, although, of course, you can talk about it together - and you should talk about it. But it is still something that every human being has to do within himself; and any so-called 'sharing' – a popular phrase these days - will not be of much help here. We can exchange information with each other about our experiences and that can help, but each person has his own task, which lies within the scope of what we then call 'I'."

"I will test this out at least, today, later … " said Raymond. "And is there any opportunity to talk about it afterwards?"

"If you want, we can talk about this again tomorrow at the same time. And then this initial look at it will indicate whether you see something in this way forward or not."

"That I see something in it," Raymond said, "I already know, although there is a lot in me that wants to ridicule it. Basically, I really do know that you are right; that it is so. And that I'm also too ambitious - though now maybe with a positive effect - not to want to be building on what I've started to get a feel for, and to become the best at it!"

Johannes and Philippe were laughing.

"That's a good impulse!" said Philippe. "Though you will find out that you are not in charge here. There are other forces at work that determine how far you will get."

"Ah," said Raymond, "that's actually true in science, too. Even in the development of software, with which I've been involved for a number of years, it's not the case that you decide for yourself how fast and effectively you want to go. There's always a difference from how you'd like it to be: one resistance after another has to be overcome, one problem after another has to be solved, and you're in an area of thought that isn't exactly pleasant. So I believe that I am well prepared to start this and give it my energy on a daily basis. Only I have one more question about God and religion, which I also asked Johannes. Isn't it necessary for us to believe in God when we go this way?"

Philippe said seriously:

"You can't impose that on a human being, you can't expect that from a human being. Modern faith no longer rests on the assumption of the existence of God, or the acceptance of the facts in the New Testament, but rests on an inner activity by which, after all, those facts - the existence of God and the truth of the Gospels - are not so much proven as simply shown.

"I would just like to say: when you become aware of God, with certainty, then of course unbelief does not endure."

"Unfortunately, I can't imagine that … " said Raymond. "What about you, Els?"

"Neither can I. We both grew up with no religious background, went to schools where there was no mention of the Bible or anything. At most, there was a reference here and there in history and they were usually heavily negative - the Crusades and that sort of thing. I've sometimes wondered what it is about the human being that tries to do the good and avoid the evil. Why would one do that? Why would you, as a doctor, want to make an effort to help people when you could earn the same amount of money in a much less intensive way? Money can't be the only thing. Actually, I don't understand it at all. If one were to assume that there is a moral world order that is good - which then coincides with God - then one could understand it. Then one would say, unconsciously one aims to stay in harmony with that moral world order. Now I believe we both live like that - although lately, listening to the principles of singularity, I have had my doubts and thought: isn't the beginning of moral action in ethical thinking? If you can have such anti-human thoughts, can you still live morally? But on the other hand, I know Raymond so well that I know that he is a thoroughly moral person. So that remains a mystery for the time being. Furthermore, of course, we accept our being simply the way it is and I don't think we have had an impulse to become more loving than we are, more truthful than we are. Moral self-education is not really a theme in our lives. I could imagine - the moment you acknowledge the existence of God, that you would want to change that … "

"I have another question … " Raymond said, "about that non-ethical area in the thought process of singularity. It is anticipated that it will be possible, just as you watch a film or play a game on the computer, you could do that within yourself and you could also change your personality in that sense. For example, you could have erotic relationships with people of your choice. If I look at that honestly, I think: I don't think that's moral anymore. But other aspects of it are attractive: the adaptability of your appearance, the revelation of your personality, the sharing of your inner life with your fellow human beings … By connecting one brain to another, you would be able to share everything you think directly. What kind of response do you have to that?"

Johannes said:

"We expect in the future - but it is still far, very far away from us - a transition to a human existence that no longer has to take place in flesh and bones and blood. Then, there will certainly be a plasticity that is impossible now, because the body in which we live is so solid and material. But in that spiritual vision of the future, let me say that that transcendental body will be connected with developed morality. That you would indulge yourself in other such bodies will be a fundamental impossibility."

"That's a topic," Raymond said, "which is very important, I think. There should be a publication on that, so that those of us who long for an existence in which the death of the physical body no longer

plays a role, can find comfort. Surely there must be somewhere one can read that in the future it will be different from what is offered by the singularity? It offers a certain consolation in a technical manner and, if you want to see some religious coherence, you can find it in the philosophy of Teilhard de Chardin. Thus, we might well imagine that we can have something like that now which, as you say, would only come much, much later. But then, it does not arise via a technical electromagnetic field, but via something that really transcends nature. If I understand it correctly, biology will also be conquered, but in a different way."

"We'll talk about that in our last conversation," Johannes said. "To-morrow we can have a conversation about your first experiences with the being of the self in thinking."

At lunch, Raymond said to Els:

"Sometimes I feel like we've ended up with a bunch of Jehovah's Witnesses … "

"What makes you think that?!?" said Els. "I've only heard mention of God and the Bible when you've brought it up yourself!"

"A cult, then. They speak of 'we believe this and we believe that.' "

"I think you're talking nonsense!" Els said. "There's no coercion, they work entirely through their own understanding, and if you can't or don't want to go along with that understanding, that's fine."

"That's true … " he said. "I also feel I'm being unreasonably willing, to always believe the sincerity of this 'collegium' and not to cherish any doubt. Surely there must be some kind of worldview behind it? Surely they must be part of some sort of group?"

"I thought," Els said, "that you were so at home on the internet! Didn't you look up this institute here in the mountains?"

"I didn't get around to it in the half hour we had available, because I kept having more and more substantial questions. But apparently you did look it up?"

"I did … " she said. "And it's very clear that these people work in a completely independent way, based on anthroposophy."

"Hey bah!" Raymond said from the bottom of his heart.

"Do you know anything about that?"

"No, but the word is familiar and has a certain aura … "

"A godless person who talks about auras! You're getting more and more interesting, Raymond! What these gentlemen and the lady have been telling us over the past few days is simply anthroposophy. I even remember that the word was once mentioned, not as a name, but as a description of what they practise here. But they do stand alone, don't belong to any association or society. They are, as it were, a society in themselves."

"Okay … Then I must become a follower of Rudolf Steiner?"

"The hallmark of anthroposophy is that it's based on the foundation of freedom. So you don't have to do anything. It's based entirely on Man's desire for freedom. Whether you want to understand what is understandable, or you turn away from that; it's okay. Whether you follow completely different ideas for a while, whether you live with thoughts that are short-lived or enduring, that go wandering or are mistaken, you can always go back to that single point of thought, which Philippe has described so beautifully and extensively. If you can acknowledge that, then you can acknowledge anthroposophy. What Philippe has explained to us are Rudolf Steiner's original ideas or findings. That is to say, of course, he does not appear as a completely independent inventor, but he bases his thinking on the thinking of great predecessors. But I am convinced that the recognition of self in thinking is the key point made by Rudolf Steiner. In particular, he shows that from that starting point another whole field of science can be built - as Philippe has so clearly explained."

"So: no Jehovah's Witnesses - but anthroposophists! You are well informed! I'm not so sure I like all this too much … "

"They make no secret of the fact that their work is the outcome of anthroposophy. But they do contend that they are developing this anthroposophy further - and therefore that they aren't just repeating Steiner mindlessly."

"Well … " said Raymond, "what does it matter! The point is indeed: does one have anything to gain from this, can one acknowledge something in it that counterbalances the promises of singularity? Or is this a castle in the sky or an illusion? As Philippe said, we'll have to find out for ourselves. And I understand that it is possible only if everyone tries this for themselves. So, I'm looking forward to this evening, when we'll have time to actually try it … "

They went for a walk, but Raymond again struggled to be fully attentive to nature; because he was excited about what he was going to do that evening ...

When at last he was sitting in his chair in the bedroom, he tried to remember exactly what Philippe had said. It was frustrating that he couldn't check the internet for the weather forecast, or to save a book to read later. He had actively to go back to what Philippe had said ...

First, he had mentioned the need to establish his *objective reality*, and then he had turned his attention inside out and pointed out the possibility of finding his own substance in the development of thought itself. He called it I, the I that unfolds thoughts and connects them with each other. So, there, you should be able to experience that you exist in reality, that it is not some conclusion drawn from other facts that brings you to the conclusive fact: 'I am'; nor the dull physical feeling that makes you know constantly that you are there, in accordance with being an external object.

So now a point had to be found where the I identified itself as its being.

Thinking these thoughts was difficult enough, he missed the handle of sensory reality, although he was used to thinking in non-sensory perceptible facts. But although the facts he was accustomed to thinking were not perceptible, they were thought of as existing in the sensory world. Now he had to become aware of himself as a thinker in such a way that this provided a sense of being.

Suddenly he remembered the recommendation to take a concept with which you work a lot, but of which you don't fully know the meaning. Like the concept: *strength*. You would then have to maintain that, and while maintaining that you would have to become aware that you are there ... .

He made an attempt ...   He experienced enormously powerful thoughts that wanted to distract him, with more or less trivial thoughts, from his point of concentration.

For a moment he managed to hold on to 'not knowing' what strength is, and in that very moment he recognized his feeling of having lost his presence of mind. At the same time, he caught a glimpse of himself as the one who was struggling to think only of strength and realizing that he did not really know it. It was so short-lived and so transient that he had no choice but to try again - and the second time nothing came of it.

Somewhat despondent, he stopped and re-joined Els. She hadn't achieved any results either - even less than Raymond. But she said:

"Well, naturally, we can't expect, coming from a completely different world, to find everything that we've been promised from active thinking straightaway, at the first glance. These people are experienced researchers in this field, they dedicate their lives to it, and we are novices, pupils at best."

Raymond said:

"It's a bit painful when you've done three degrees, you pass cum laude, you get your PhD cum laude and you're invited to become a professor - and then you come out here to some remote place in the mountains where there are some interesting and impressive men and women, who draw your attention to the locus that has a direct connection with intelligence … and you're completely empty-handed!"

"You could choose *not* to see it that way! You could also say: it is sad that I've never met anyone before who has pointed out to me that there is anything other than the external sensory world, which is so besieged by science that it has to reveal its secrets right down to the very smallest particles! Apparently there exists another locus, and that locus is apparently connected with my own life, where something is active in my inner being, which generates the whole of this scientific development, but which itself is never considered at all! Isn't that sad? What kind of world is this that makes extensive use of a quality, without ever wondering what that quality is actually based on?"

"Yes, but we do wonder! That is precisely this Human Brain Project, the desire to want to know how intelligence works!"

"But utterly outwardly!" Els exclaimed. "And you notice, when you look inside, you can't even sustain yourself there, you have so little power to sustain yourself outside the thinking that stays awake with the senses. It is then only natural and self-evident that we are, let's just say, infants, who first need a nurturer so that we can gradually be and know ourselves in that completely overlooked, unknown world."

"That really is fantastic Els!' said Raymond.

"Are you making fun of me now?" she asked.

"No, I really mean it … You have a real talent for developing that aspect, you fit in really well with these people here … "

"And so do you!" she said obstinately.

"I have to deal with my own arrogance, my dear Els, I know that; and the arrogance of the intellect is a difficult thing to overcome. But I can see it, and you mustn't blame me if I rebel on a regular basis, because I went in a certain direction and had gone a long way down that road. Suddenly there's a voice saying: Get off! It doesn't lead to the good, it doesn't lead to the truth, it probably doesn't even lead to anything beautiful!

"Then everything I've done has been for nothing - a big mistake."

"No!" Els said determinedly. "You have been training your intelligence very intensively, that must be reflected when you delve into the realm of intelligence itself."

"Well, with this poor result we'll go back to Philippe tomorrow … "

"Yesterday I was discouraged," Raymond said to Philippe. "It is true that for a moment I observed something of an activity in thinking and perhaps even in being myself, but so short-lived, so ephemeral and so disturbed by all the everyday thoughts - and also by rebellious feelings - that I have not got any further. When I woke up this morning, I thought: I could imagine that one could bring that locus that revealed itself to me for a moment - and then completely disappeared into invisibility - into full clear consciousness. Then one would be able to think with clear self-awareness that everything one perceives - yes, let's just say - is gaining strength … But it is a hopeful picture with a kind of logical foundation. I don't know if it's a real possibility that I could ever get that far."

"Actually, you shouldn't even ask yourself that," said Philippe. "When you realise that it might be important to try to bring this point into consciousness over and over again, it's actually enough that you practise it. You shouldn't want to have a goal, the goal is the activity itself, and in that activity lies the result. It is like a flower unfolding: everything is already in bud, but the development is yet to come … "

"I believe that now I must make my own examination both of the books you have published and the work of Rudolf Steiner, and then, when I have found in them some firm ground beneath my feet, perhaps I can come back to you to teach me how I should proceed.

"I will leave here with a good impression: in the first place, nature which impresses one so awesomely here, with science in the background, trying strenuously to understand and imitate and improve nature's Majesty. And secondly, in the midst of nature lies your activity, and It opens up an unprecedented world, of which I can now only imagine a few pitiful representations. But when I observe you, interact with you, speak to you and understand you, it is of course not so difficult to see that *what* you are proclaiming must be true. Apart from the fact that I seem to see it myself, you are proclaiming the existence of a world even larger than nature. I feel an unprecedented urge to go as far into that world as is possible. So I cannot ignore this visit to you and continue on my old path. My life has completely changed. For Els, that is less the case - if I may speak for her - because she is already so much more in such a world of thoughts and feelings. Maybe that's easier for a doctor too, because you're constantly confronted with that aspect of human nature. So, I can't go back and I am wondering how to proceed. I believe that you have given us what is possible at this moment; but, how to proceed?"

At this point Johannes responded:

"I touched on that yesterday. You asked the question about publicising how, from such awareness of self in thought, a very concrete experience can arise of the development that humanity will go through and which will, eventually - in the course of thousands of years, admittedly - make it possible for an evolved human being to live on earth without being hindered by a heavy material physical body - even also without being hindered by the phenomenon of being born and dying.

"It would really be an honour for me, Raymond, if I had the opportunity to present this vision of the future to you, which is thus similar to singularity, but which is a purely spiritual vision much further away in time. I would then invite you to participate in our - as you call it – Collegium for a few weeks and to record what Philippe and I would like to present to this Collegium. We don't really want to do that anymore without you and Els being present."

Raymond bowed his head. He sighed deeply and said:

"Where does this honour come from? This wanderer and doubter doesn't deserve this at all!"

Johannes didn't contradict him and Philip kept silent. A depth opened up between them. They let it sink in until Johannes broke the silence and said:

"We, the Master, Eve, Beato, Philippe, Peter and I, we would very much appreciate it if you would come to listen and understand what Philippe and I would like to describe about the future of Man when he is no longer bound to a physical body."

Again, a silence fell until it was broken by Raymond with the words;

" Good, isn't it, Els? We'll be there!"

Els nodded ...

In half sleep Els saw the labyrinth again. It seemed flooded, great waves came out and suddenly she saw, swallowed up by the waves, the dead monster emerging.

But where was Raymond?

"Here I am!" he said. "I've been out of here a long time. I was out before we got to the mountains, otherwise I wouldn't have got to the mountains at all. You should know, Els, time runs the other way around here ... What's cause is effect and what's effect is cause."

He was just lying next to her in bed, he was asleep; he couldn't possibly have said anything, and yet it was he who said this to her ...

They were sitting at the table in their apartment in Amsterdam.

This was where it had all started … Here she had put her iPhone on the table to record what he had to say about his life. And even though you couldn't say that dictating it was the cause, the result changed their lives completely.

It was impossible to say exactly what it was like, but now that they were back here, they both knew for sure that Raymond's self-reflection had been the beginning. He wanted to write down how the life of a gifted man goes.

Now they were back here … Everything was exactly the same and yet nothing was the same. They had an indescribable wealth with them. Maybe they used to have it, too, but not consciously. That's why Raymond's fear of ending up at home on his old track proved unfounded. The lessons there, high up in the mountains, had been so intensive that it was as if they had been baptized and had received a new life impulse.

There was no religious mood, or maybe they had a one-sided view of it …

They sat together at the table to draw up a text for the invitations to their wedding. That, too, was a turning point in their lives; it had never seemed as if a marriage would come about.

When they were finished, Els said:

"How are we going to carry on with what we started there in the mountains? After all, we're all alone here."

"One thing is clear," said Raymond, "I'm not going to join some society. The connection with that group over there in the mountains should be enough and, in any case, we already have an appointment for this summer. Over the next two months I want to study intensively myself and practise thinking in the way Philippe has done. I have to say that I really feel like it, because it is something that is completely new and for which you can fully commit yourself again with a kind of childlike enthusiasm.

"We have each other … Two should be enough - that's something very different from being alone! We can discuss everything we experience with each other; after all, we are, as it turns out, real partners in this area."

"I hope I can find the energy to do that … " Els said. "You now have a few months' rest to prepare for your new task, so you can fit this in very well. But my work with patients continues."

"It seems very good to me," Raymond said, "to try to expose that inner world to all those resistances. After all, it's a tremendous resistance, the earth's existence. Your brain, blood circulation, organs, everything gets in the way. And all that is actually appreciated more than the real locus of human intelligence – which can, apparently, function without using all those billions of neurons and synapses and such! That was my first field of research, in which I was so incredibly happy. The brain must now be forgotten with all its power, it must be illumined … Day by day my interest in this is growing, day by day I also feel that it is a great undertaking'.

Els said;

"Even your looks have changed, Raymond. You were that kind of intellectual bean-pole. Now you're starting to get heavier, not fatter, but you are starting to look more like men like Philippe and Johannes with whom, of course, it's not the body size that impresses, because they're both slim. But a certain willpower - devoured in the intellectual by all those synapses, I'd say - is now becoming evident in your stature, your presence."

"I don't think that's bad for an aspiring professor … " Raymond smiled. "I've always felt like the smartest, but not the strongest."

"Let's just keep quiet about this with our friends for now, Raymond, until perhaps one day the time will come when that other locus will be strong enough. Otherwise, I fear that we'd trample on our budding powers with all the arguments and counterarguments."

"Then we'll remain just the two of us and get nourishment from the mountains once in a while …

" 'What greater gain in life can Man e'er know
Than when God-Nature will to him explain?
How into Spirit steadfastness may flow,
How steadfast, too, the Spirit-Born remain.'[4]

"Now I see that in all my desire for knowledge I have always searched for this revelation in nature. But because you are unaware of this other way of thinking, you don't know God and you don't even know that you are looking for Him."

"We will look for Him!" Els said.

---

[4] Goethe, Poems: Lines on Seeing Schiller's Skull, 1826. Translation from 'The Works of JW von Goethe, by George Henry Lewes and others, 1856
['What more can Man gain in life than that God-Nature reveals himself to him … How she (Nature) makes the solid dissolve into spirit, how she firmly preserves what has been born by the spirit']

Bibliography / References:

Ray Kurzweil, The singularity is near / Menschheit 2.0, Lola Verlag 2005.

Interview with Ray Kurzweil on Instapundit.com, 2005.

Roger Penrose, The Emperor's New Mind, OUP, 1989

[De nieuwe Geest van de keizer, Amsterdam 1990].

Pierre Teilhard de Chardin,   The Phenomenon of Man, 1955.
                                Christianity and Evolution,1968.
                                The Future of Man, 2004.

Marsilio Ficino, über die Liebe oder Platons Gastmahl.
Felix Meiner Verlag 2014.

Joel Frohlich, Reverse Engineering the Brain, psychologytoday.com

The Human Brain Project, humanbrainproject.eu

The Blue Brain Project, bluebrain.epfl.ch

Singularity University, SU.org

Robert A. Freitas Jr., Nanomedicine, Nanomedicine.com

Kevin Warwick, kevinwarwick.com. See also the videos on YouTube.

Rudolf Steiner, Philosophy und Anthroposophy, Collected Works 35.